GRAMMAR AND BEYOND

WORKBOOK

Lawrence J. Zwier

Harry Holden

CAMBRIDGE UNIVERSITY PRESS
Cambridge, New York, Melbourne, Madrid, Cape Town,
Singapore, São Paulo, Delhi, Tokyo, Mexico City

Cambridge University Press
32 Avenue of the Americas, New York, NY 10013-2473, USA

www.cambridge.org
Information on this title: www.cambridge.org/9780521279925

© Cambridge University Press 2012

First published 2012

Printed in the United States of America

A catalog record for this publication is available from the British Library.

ISBN 978-0-521-14296-0 Student's Book 2
ISBN 978-0-521-14310-3 Student's Book 2A
ISBN 978-0-521-14312-7 Student's Book 2B
ISBN 978-0-521-27991-8 Workbook 2
ISBN 978-0-521-27992-5 Workbook 2A
ISBN 978-0-521-27993-2 Workbook 2B
ISBN 978-1-107-67653-4 Teacher Support Resource with CD-ROM 2
ISBN 978-0-521-14335-6 Class Audio CD 2
ISBN 978-1-139-06186-5 Writing Skills Interactive 2

Art direction and layout services: TSI Graphics

Contents

PART 5 Adjectives, Adverbs, and Prepositions

Simple Present

Are You Often Online?

Simple Present

1 Complete the paragraph with the simple present form of the verbs in parentheses. Some verbs are negative.

Fernanda and I _are_ (be) from Guatemala, but we _____ (not live)
    (1)   (2)

there now. We _____ (live) in Houston with our two children. Fernanda's parents
              (3)

_____ (not be) with us in Texas, but Fernanda _____ (stay) in touch
        (4)   (5)

with them online. Every day, she _____ (communicate) by e-mail with
                                      (6)

her parents and _____ (send) them a lot of pictures of their grandchildren. We
                (7)

_____ (not go) back home very often because plane tickets _____ (be)
        (8)   (9)

expensive. Fernanda's parents _____ (not travel) to Houston often. As a
                                      (10)

result, Fernanda rarely _____ (see) them. I rarely _____ (see) my parents, either.
                        (11)   (12)

Fernanda and I _____ (miss) our families and friends in Guatemala a lot.
               (13)

2 A Read the social network profiles of Na and Ben. Unscramble the words to write questions. Use the simple present form of the verbs. Then answer the questions.

	Na Liu	Ben Seeley
Name:	Na Liu	Ben Seeley
Hometown:	Beijing, China	San Diego, CA
Employer:	San Diego High School	Triton Software
Activities:	practice yoga every day	swim twice a week
About me:	married to Ming, 1 child, no pets	married to Ellen, 3 children, no pets
Favorite kinds of TV programs:	reality shows, game shows	sitcoms, dramas

1. from / be / Na / Where ?

   Q: _Where is Na from?_

   A: _She is from Beijing, China._

2. Ben / China / from / Be ?

   Q: _Is Ben from China?_

   A: _No, he isn't. He's from San Diego._

3. Ben and Ellen / How many / children / have ?

   Q: _____

   A: _____

4. yoga / practice / Who ?

   Q: _____

   A: _____

5. do / Ben / What / twice a week ?

   Q: _____

   A: _____

6. reality shows / Do / Na / like ?

   Q: _____

   A: _____

B Write more questions and answers about Na and Ben.

1. **Q:** _Where does Na work?_

   A: _She works at San Diego High School._

2. **Q:** _____

   A: _____

3. **Q:** _____

   A: _____

3 A Write simple present questions or answers about the things Lisa, Tom, Eric, and Tatiana do online. Use *How often* and the information in the chart.

Activity	Lisa and Tom	Eric	Tatiana
read the news online	often	every day	always
get map directions online	frequently	rarely	occasionally
pay bills online	twice a month	hardly ever	once a month
watch TV programs online	sometimes	often	seldom
compare prices online	rarely	always	sometimes

1. **Q:** How often do Lisa and Tom pay bills online?

   A: *Lisa and Tom pay bills online twice a month.*

2. **Q:** *How often does Eric get map directions online?*

   A: Eric rarely gets map directions online.

3. **Q:** How often do Lisa and Tom read the news online?

   A: _____

4. **Q:** _____

   A: Lisa and Tom sometimes watch TV programs online.

5. **Q:** How often does Eric pay bills online?

   A: _____

6. **Q:** _____

   A: Eric reads the news online every day.

7. **Q:** How often does Tatiana watch TV programs online?

   A: _____

8. **Q:** _____

   A: Tatiana sometimes compares prices online.

B Answer the questions with information that is true for you.

1. How often do you read the news online?   *I occasionally read the news online.*

2. How often do you get map directions online?   _____

3. How often do you pay bills online?   _____

4. How often do you watch TV programs online?   _____

5. How often do you compare prices online?   _____

Time Clauses and Factual Conditionals

1 Read the sentences about Pruitt Community College's online registration process. Circle the correct word or phrase.

1. **When** / **While** students are ready to register for classes, they go to the school's website.

2. Students need a user account **as soon as** / **before** they register online.

3. **After** / **If** they don't have a user account, the school gives them one.

4. **As soon as** / **Before** they have an account, students begin to sign up for classes.

5. Students click "Select Class" **while** / **when** they choose a class.

6. **Before** / **After** they click "Select Class," the class appears on their schedule.

7. **While** / **Before** students click "Finish Enrolling," they should check their schedule carefully.

8. Students can register online **before** / **while** they are at school or at home.

2 Read the information about buying products online. Combine the condition with the main clause in two ways using *if* and *when*. Add commas when necessary.

Condition	Main Clause
1. Bob / want / a good product	he / read / the customer reviews section
2. Ted and Ana / want / the best prices	they / compare / prices at different sites
3. Stacy / not need / a product quickly	she / not pay / extra for fast shipping
4. David / not be / sure about a product	he / read / the return policy first
5. Bill / not have / enough information	he / call / the store
6. Karen / use / a credit card	she / make / sure the site is secure

1. If *Bob wants a good product, he reads the customer reviews section*   .

   Bob reads the customer reviews section   if *he wants a good product*   .

2. If _____ .

   _____ if _____ .

3. When _____ .

   _____ when _____ .

4. If _____ .

   _____ if _____ .

5. If _____ .

   _____ if _____ .

6. When _____ .

   _____ when _____ .

3 Think about how you buy a product online. Complete the sentences with information that is true for you.

1. If I want to buy a product online, I *look at several websites*   .

2. After that, I _____ .

3. I often _____ while _____ .

4. Whenever I _____ , I _____ .

Avoid Common Mistakes

1 Circle the mistakes.

1. **A:** How (online games do) harm people? **B:** If people **don't** play too **much**, they should
                (a)   (b)   (c)

   be fine.

2. **When** children start to play online **games some** parents worry. Other parents **don't** worry.
    (a)   (b)   (c)

3. A player **does** not **sometimes** interact with other players. Some games **do** not have
              (a)   (b)   (c)

   multiple players.

4. **While** they are **online** people **sometimes watch TV shows**.
    (a)   (b)   (c)

5. Some games need many players. If a player **does** not **sometimes** help the **others**, they
                                               (a)   (b)   (c)

   all lose.

6. **Sometimes** players **does** not meet in person, but they **do** become friends.
     (a)   (b)   (c)

7. Personally, I **amn't** against online games. **Sometimes** they **do** teach valuable skills.
               (a)   (b)   (c)

8. **A:** When **online games do** help people? **B:** If games use special **skills**, children **learn**
                 (a)   (b)   (c)

   new things.

2 Find and correct eight more mistakes in the paragraph about taking online classes.

    I'm a community college student, but ~~I amn't~~ *I'm not* in a classroom. I doesn't live near the

college campus. Where I do take my classes? They are all online, so I take classes at home

on my computer. As soon as one of my teachers posts a lesson online I get an e-mail

about the assignment. When I finish the assignment I send my homework to my teacher

in an e-mail. She don't usually see her students, but she interacts with us online. I don't

sometimes understand an assignment, so I talk to her online. We also have a discussion

board where we post comments to other students. I really doesn't miss going to classes on

campus. This is so much more peaceful! I amn't so tired after class this way.

Self-Assessment

Circle the word or phrase that correctly completes each sentence.

1. How much time _____ you spend on the Internet?

   a. are   b. does   c. do

2. _____ they worried about the time they spend online?

   a. Is   b. Are   c. Do

3. People _____ about the effects of technology on our lives.

   a. aren't agree   b. disagrees   c. disagree

4. Angela _____ usually think about online security.

   a. doesn't   b. don't   c. no

5. Mike almost always finishes his work _____ he leaves the office.

   a. while   b. before   c. during

6. How _____ you spend your time online?

   a. do   b. are   c. does

7. Ahmed works from home four days a week. He _____ goes to his office.

   a. usually   b. often   c. seldom

8. Tasha _____ e-mail while she is on vacation.

   a. never checks   b. don't check   c. doesn't checks

9. Susan never spends time on social networking sites _____ she is at work.

   a. during   b. while   c. as soon as

10. I sometimes text my sister _____ she doesn't answer her phone.

    a. if   b. while   c. before

11. Mei _____ a good wireless connection on her cell phone.

    a. doesn't sometimes get   b. don't get sometimes   c. sometimes doesn't get

12. Their children usually _____ video games online.

    a. do plays   b. plays   c. play

13. How _____ online students interact with each other?

    a. are   b. do   c. does

14. I _____ read the news online. I read it twice a week.

    a. never   b. occasionally   c. always

15. _____ I change it immediately.

    a. If I forget my password,   b. If I forget my password   c. I forget my password,

Present Progressive and Simple Present

Brainpower

Present Progressive

1 Complete the sentences with the present progressive form of the verbs in parentheses.

1. These days, scientists _are doing_ research on the effects of physical exercise on the brain.
   (do)

2. They _____ how exercise helps brain functions.
   (study)

3. While you exercise, you _____ more blood to the heart and to your brain.
   (send)

4. During this process, your brain _____ more chemicals for healthy brain activity.
   (produce)

5. This means that your brain _____ hundreds of thousands of new cells.
   (grow)

6. These new cells _____ the brain's mental abilities stronger.
   (make)

7. They _____ memory and learning ability.
   (improve)

8. These are just a few of the changes that happen when you _____ .
   (exercise)

2 Write questions and answers about what Yesenia is doing these days to keep her brain healthy. Use the present progressive.

1. What / Yesenia / do / to stay fit?

Q: *What's Yesenia doing to stay fit?*

A: *She's jogging.*

2. Yesenia / eat / breakfast?

Q: *Is Yesenia eating breakfast?*

A: _____

3. Yesenia / walk to work?

Q: _____

A: _____

4. Yesenia / watch TV / in the evenings?

Q: _____

A: _____

5. Yesenia / do crossword puzzles?

Q: _____

A: _____

6. What / Yesenia / do before bed?

Q: _____

A: _____

3 Unscramble the sentences. Use the present progressive.

1. My friends and I / to exercise our brains / do new things

   My friends and I are doing new things to exercise our brains.

2. learn / I / Portuguese

   _____

3. write / Glenn and Bruce / with their opposite hands

   _____

4. on a different road to work / Greg / drive

   _____

5. board games / play / Ingrid and I

   _____

6. Natalya / yoga and meditation / study

   _____

7. play / Bingo these days / Luis

   _____

8. Dustin and Sharon / a lot more / read

   _____

9. our new hobbies / enjoy / We

   _____

4 What are you doing to keep your brain healthy? Write sentences that are true for you.

1. *I am doing crossword puzzles.* _____

2. _____

3. _____

Simple Present and Present Progressive Compared

1 A Complete the paragraph with the verbs in parentheses. Use the simple present or present progressive.

Some children _____learn_____ (learn) only one language at home, but Sofia Moreno
(1)

_____ (learn) two languages at the age of three. Diego and Paula Moreno both
(2)

_____ (speak) Spanish and English. They _____ (want) their
(3)   (4)

daughter to speak both languages, too. As a result, Paula always _____ (talk) to
(5)

Sofia in Spanish, and Diego only _____ (use) English with their daughter. Right
(6)

now, they _____ (get) Sofia ready for bed. Diego often _____
(7)   (8)

(sing) a song in English that American parents _____ (sing) to their children at
(9)

bedtime. But tonight, Paula _____ (read) Sofia a story in Spanish. Most scientists
(10)

_____ (agree) that these are good ways for children to learn two languages.
(11)

B Write questions or answers. Use the information in A.

1. **Q:** What is Sofia learning at home? **A:** *Sofia is learning two languages.* _____

2. **Q:** What does Paula speak to Sofia? **A:** _____

3. **Q:** _____ **A:** He speaks English to Sofia.

4. **Q:** Who is getting Sofia ready for bed now? **A:** _____

5. **Q:** _____ **A:** He often sings Sofia a song
in English.

6. **Q:** What is Paula doing right now? **A:** _____

7. **Q:** _____ **A:** Yes, scientists agree that these are
good ways.

2 Complete the sentences. Use the simple present or present progressive form of the verbs in
parentheses.

1. Older people with active lives _*have*_ (have) an advantage.

2. The advantage _____ (be) a healthier brain.

3. My parents still _____ (want) to learn new things.

4. My dad _____ (look) for a running partner.

5. My mom _____ (think) about taking a karate class.

6. My grandmother _____ (know) how to garden.

7. My grandfather _____ (want) to learn how to play tennis.

8. My grandparents _____ (believe) that active lives
keep them healthy.

9. I _____ (love) all the things my family can do.

Avoid Common Mistakes

1 Circle the mistakes.

1. These days, people **are living** longer because they (**taking**) care of themselves.
   (a)   (b)   (c)

2. What changes **are** people **make** to their lifestyles? Are these changes **working**?
   (a)   (b)   (c)

3. Most people **are wanting to keep** their hearts healthy. They **are exercising** more
   (a)   (b)   (c)
   these days.

4. Three times a week, I **am going** to a gym to **exercise**. I **lift** weights and swim.
   (a)   (b)   (c)

5. My spouse and I are **planing** healthier meals, too. We **are** not **eating** junk food.
   (a)   (b)   (c)

6. We **are enjoing** a board game **right now** with our friends.
   (a) (b)   (c)

7. Scientists **aren't understanding** everything about the brain, but they **are**
   (a)   (b)
   making progress.
   (c)

8. These days, they **are studying** the human brain, and they **doing** research **to learn** more.
   (a)   (b)   (c)

2 Find and correct seven more mistakes in the paragraph about improving your memory.

behaving
Are you ~~behave~~ differently than you normally do? Are you experiencing sudden changes in mood now? Are you having trouble with decisions? Are you wanting someone else to make decisions for you? If you answer yes to these questions, maybe your memory getting worse. Doctors are thinking a few simple changes in lifestyle can help improve your memory. It working for Joe Jones. These days, he is eat more fruits and vegetables. He sleeping more than before. Also, he is enjoing life more. He often connects with friends on social networking sites. He is 63 years old, and his brain and body are in excellent condition.

Self-Assessment

Circle the word or phrase that correctly completes each sentence.

1. Right now, Paul _____ a TV program about the human brain.

   a. is watch   b. watches   c. is watching

2. Doctors _____ that learning a new skill improves the brain.

   a. are thinking   b. think   c. thinking

3. These days, _____ to learn new skills.

   a. I try   b. I trying   c. I'm trying

4. My grandparents _____ a walk at the moment.

   a. are taking   b. takes   c. take

5. Every morning, Annette _____ vitamins.

   a. is takeing   b. takes   c. taking

6. Patricia _____ with her parents now.

   a. living   b. is living   c. live

7. I _____ to borrow your computer right now.

   a. needing   b. am needing   c. need

8. Carol and her husband _____ a vacation to relax their minds.

   a. are planning   b. are planing   c. plan

9. He _____ to do crossword puzzles on Sunday mornings.

   a. is liking   b. is likeing   c. likes

10. Gina can't answer the phone. She _____ her teeth.

    a. is brushing   b. brushing   c. brushes

11. Joon-Sung and his wife always _____ their seat belts when they are in the car.

    a. wears   b. are wearing   c. wear

12. _____ for your glasses? They're on the table in the kitchen.

    a. You looking   b. Are you looking   c. Do you look

13. This is a great class. We really _____ it!

    a. are enjoying   b. are enjoing   c. enjoys

14. This week _____ memory in our psychology class.

    a. we studying   b. we study   c. we're studying

15. What _____ to improve your brainpower?

    a. you doing   b. you are doing   c. are you doing

Imperatives

What's Appropriate?

Imperatives

1 Complete the advice for job interviews. Use the affirmative or negative imperatives of the verbs in the box.

arrive	be	dress	learn	send
ask	chew	forget	listen	thank

1. _____*Learn*_____ about the company before the interview.

2. __*Don't arrive*__ late for the interview.

3. _____ appropriately in a business suit.

4. _____ to bring copies of your résumé.

5. _____ polite to everyone at the company.

6. _____ carefully to the interviewer's questions.

7. _____ gum during the interview.

8. _____ questions about the company and the position during the interview.

9. _____ the interviewer for the interview when you are finished.

10. _____ the interviewer a short thank-you e-mail after the interview.

2 Write sentences with time clauses or *if* clauses about keeping children safe on social networking sites. Use the words in parentheses and the imperative form of the verbs. Add commas when necessary.

1. your child / join a social networking site   discuss / the rules for using the site

   (before) _Before your child joins a social networking site, discuss the rules for using_

   the site.

2. your child / use the site   talk / about cyberbullying with him or her

   (before) _____

3. your child / post / a photo   check / that it doesn't show personal information

   (when) _____

4. you / be / worried about your child's safety   buy / an app that monitors him or her

   (if) _____

5. your child / read / gossip   explain / that gossip can hurt people

   (when) _____

6. you / see / something inappropriate on your child's page   talk / to your child about it

   (if) _____

3 Write sentences about what is appropriate to do in the classroom. Use the imperative.

Affirmative

1. _Always listen to the teacher when she is speaking._

2. _____

3. _____

4. _____

Negative

5. _____

6. _____

7. _____

8. _____

Let's . . .

1 Tam and Ahn are going to a graduation party. Complete the conversation with *Let's* or *Let's not* and the imperative form of the verbs in parentheses.

Ahn: I don't know what to wear to Diana's graduation party.

Tam: Well, I think it's a formal party. *Let's wear* (wear) some really nice clothes.
(1)

Ahn: OK. What time is the party?

Tam: It starts at 6:00 p.m., but _____ (arrive) too early.
(2)

Ahn: I agree. I don't like to be the first one there. _____ (wrap) her present now.
(3)

Tam: Which wrapping paper should I use?

Ahn: _____ (use) the gold paper. _____ (forget) to sign the card.
(4)   (5)

Tam: OK. Are they serving food at the party?

Ahn: I don't know. _____ (eat) something before we go.
(6)

Tam: Good idea!

2 A group of students is making a class blog. Write sentences with *Let's* or *Let's not*.

1. (decide on a topic) *Let's decide on a topic.* _____

2. (find a site for our blog) _____

3. (read the blog site's guidelines) _____

4. (write an entry every week) _____

5. (take turns responding to comments) _____

6. (make grammar or spelling mistakes) _____

7. (check comments for inappropriate language) _____

8. (give personal information) _____

9. (make a survey for the blog) _____

10. (write entries that are too long) _____

Avoid Common Mistakes

1 Circle the mistakes.

1. **Take** the placement test in the testing center. (**Dont**) **go** to the registrar.
   (a)   (b)   (c)

2. **Leave** personal items such as backpacks at home. **Donot bring** them to the
   (a)   (b)   (c)

   testing center.

3. **Show** your driver's license. If you **don't have** a license, **no** worry. Show your passport.
   (a)   (b)   (c)

4. If you forget to turn off your phone, and it rings, **donot answer** it. **Give** it to the teacher.
                                                        (a)   (b)   (c)

5. If you have a question, **ask** a testing center employee. **Dont talk** to other students.
                           (a)   (b)   (c)

6. **Make** sure you answer the questions **completely**. **No** leave out anything important.
   (a)   (b)   (c)

7. **Donot forget** to put your name on your test paper. **Check** it before you hand it in.
   (a)   (b)   (c)

8. Finally, **let's make** this a good testing experience. **Lets not break** the rules.
              (a)   (b)   (c)

2 Find and correct seven more mistakes in the paragraph about the behavior of U.S. college students.

   American college students often behave very informally. However, ~~donot~~ *do not* think that there are no rules in college classrooms. Lets remember these suggestions for a positive experience in your classes. Dont come late to class. If you can't get to class on time, change to a different class time. Also, donot leave the classroom before class is over. If you have to leave, tell your teacher beforehand. No talk while the professor is talking. Your classmates want to hear the lecture and the instructions for any assignments. No answer your cell phone in class. Remember to put your cell phone on vibrate. Some professors allow drinks in class, but donot eat in the classroom. Finally, if you are not sure if a behavior is appropriate for the classroom, dont do it. Ask the professor before or after class if it is OK.

Self-Assessment

Circle the word or phrase that correctly completes each sentence.

1. _____ your cell phone before the meeting starts.

   a. Turning off   b. Turn off   c. Turn

2. _____ people before 9:00 a.m. You don't know if they are sleeping.

   a. No call   b. Donot call   c. Don't call

3. Always _____ your e-mails for mistakes before you send them out.

   a. don't check   b. checking   c. check

4. _____ e-mail the professor again. She doesn't like that.

   a. Let's not   b. Lets no   c. Lets not

5. If you get to the theater before I do, wait outside. _____ in before I get there.

   a. Donot go   b. No go   c. Don't go

6. _____ an appointment to see the doctor if you don't feel better by tomorrow.

   a. Makes   b. Make   c. Making

7. Never _____ a text message during class.

   a. send   b. sending   c. sends

8. _____ stop talking now and get our work done.

   a. Lets   b. Let   c. Let's

9. _____ on your cell phone while you're driving. It's dangerous.

   a. No talk   b. Do not talk   c. Not talking

10. When Caroline calls, _____ a message. I'm in an important meeting.

    a. taking   b. take   c. never takes

11. The meeting is starting. _____ please sit down.

    a. Everybody   b. Somebody   c. Someone

12. Lisa, _____ think of a good title for our report.

    a. let's   b. let   c. lets

13. When you go on that social networking site, _____ careful who you chat with.

    a. are   b. is   c. be

14. _____ your supervisor when you are ready to go to lunch.

    a. Tell   b. Telling   c. No telling

15. _____ talk in the movie theater. It's impolite.

    a. Let's no   b. Let's not   c. Lets no

Simple Past

Entrepreneurs

Simple Past

1 Write the verbs in the box in the correct category. Then write the simple past forms.

apply	begin	employ	get	leave	move	study	try
become	design	find	go	meet	start	teach	work

<table>
<tr><td colspan="2" align="center">Regular Verbs</td><td colspan="2" align="center">Irregular Verbs</td></tr>
<tr><td align="center">Base Form</td><td align="center">Simple Past</td><td align="center">Base Form</td><td align="center">Simple Past</td></tr>
<tr><td>1. apply</td><td>applied</td><td>1. become</td><td>became</td></tr>
<tr><td>2.</td><td></td><td>2.</td><td></td></tr>
<tr><td>3.</td><td></td><td>3.</td><td></td></tr>
<tr><td>4.</td><td></td><td>4.</td><td></td></tr>
<tr><td>5.</td><td></td><td>5.</td><td></td></tr>
<tr><td>6.</td><td></td><td>6.</td><td></td></tr>
<tr><td>7.</td><td></td><td>7.</td><td></td></tr>
<tr><td>8.</td><td></td><td>8.</td><td></td></tr>
</table>

2 Complete the conversation with the simple past form of the verbs in parentheses.

Marisa: Steven, we work together, but I don't know much about you. Where _did_ you _go_ (go)
(1)   (1)

to college?

Steven: I _____ (attend) South Falls Community College. I
(2)

_____ (graduate) last May.
(3)

Marisa: What _____ you _____ (study) there?
(4)   (4)

Steven: At first, I _____ (major) in psychology. Then I _____ (change)
(5)   (6)

to business administration. I _____ (not like) the psychology courses
(7)

very much. I _____ (want) to get some skills to start my own business.
(8)

Marisa: That's really cool, Steven.

3 Read the profile of two young entrepreneurs. Write *Yes / No* and information questions. Then answer the questions. Use the simple past.

These days, successful entrepreneurs can be any age. Elise and Evan Macmillan, brother and sister, started a gourmet chocolate business called the Chocolate Farm when they were 12 and 15 years old. They began to make chocolate from their home in Denver, Colorado. They made it in different shapes with a farm theme. At first, they sold their chocolate products to family and friends. Evan designed an amazing company website, and they won the Ernst & Young Entrepreneur of the Year Award in 1999. Because of the reputation[1] of their delicious chocolate, the business grew. The profits from their company helped pay for their college educations. In 2009, the Macmillans sold their business.

[1]**reputation:** what people say or think about something or someone

1. What / business / Elise and Evan Macmillan / start?

   Q: *What business did Elise and Evan Macmillan start?*

   A: *They started a gourmet chocolate business.*

2. Be / Elise and Evan / brother and sister?

   Q: *Were Elise and Evan brother and sister?*

   A: *Yes, they were.*

3. How / old / be / they?

   Q: _____

   A: _____

4. Where / they / live?

   Q: _____

   A: _____

5. Elise and Evan / sell / to family and friends?

   Q: _____

   A: _____

6. Elise / design / the company website?

   Q: _____

   A: _____

Simple Past of *Be* and *There Was/There Were*

1 Read the paragraph about the creator of eBay. Complete the sentences with *was, wasn't, were,* or *weren't.*

Pierre Morad Omidyar began eBay, Inc., a well-known Internet auction site. Individuals and businesses buy and sell all kinds of items on eBay. Pierre started his Internet website business when he was 28 years old. He was born in France in 1967 to Iranian parents. His father studied medicine and his mother studied languages. They brought Pierre to the United States in 1973. When Pierre graduated from Tufts University, he worked for a computer company as a programmer. In 1991, he started a software company with three friends. In 1995, Pierre started Auction Web, which became eBay, Inc., in 1997. He believed that most people were honest and that they would trade honestly. eBay was such a success that Pierre Omidyar became a billionaire and started a foundation to give away some of his money.

1. Pierre Omidyar __*was*__ born in France.

2. His parents _____ from Iran.

3. His father _____ a doctor.

4. His mother _____ an entrepreneur.

5. His family moved to the United States in 1973. Pierre _____ six years old.

6. Pierre _____ a scientist.

7. Pierre _____ a computer programmer.

8. Pierre _____ 28 years old when he started eBay.

9. Pierre believed that people _____ dishonest.

10. eBay _____ a successful company.

2 A Complete the interview with an entrepreneur. Use *there was* (*not*) or *there were* (*not*). Use contractions when possible.

Interviewer: When you started your company, __*there weren't*__ many women in business.

(1)

Margaret: No, _____ very few women with their own business. Most

(2)

women didn't work outside the home.

Interviewer: I hope _____ support from your family then.

(3)

Margaret: Oh, yes, _____ . My husband helped me with my idea and

(4)

_____ friends helping me, too.

(5)

Interviewer: What was the company you started?

Margaret: Well, in those days _____ any soft toys for babies.
(6)

_____ only hard toys. I designed and made soft toys.
(7)

Interviewer: Was your idea successful?

Margaret: Not in the beginning. People thought _____ any need for
(8)

soft toys.

Interviewer: What did you do then?

Margaret: New ideas sometimes take time. A women's magazine had an article

about my products. Suddenly, _____ a big response. Babies
(9)

loved the toys. Mothers loved them, too.

B Complete the *Yes / No* questions. Then write short answers. Use the information in A.

1. **Q:** _____*Were there*_____ many women in business?

   A: _*No, there weren't.*_

2. **Q:** _____ support from Margaret's family?

   A: _____

3. **Q:** _____ soft toys for babies then?

   A: _____

4. **Q:** _____ hard toys for babies then?

   A: _____

5. **Q:** _____ a big response after the magazine article?

   A: _____

Avoid Common Mistakes

1 Circle the mistakes.

1. Joanna **last week** **went** to the library. She **needed** a book about famous millionaires.
   (a)   (b)   (c)

2. I **did** a search yesterday. **There were** a new website for young **entrepreneurs**.
   (a)   (b)   (c)

3. **In 2010**, Ahmed **visits** his **company's** offices in California, New Jersey, and Illinois.
   (a)   (b)   (c)

4. **When** they first **met**, they **didn't got** along.
   (a)   (b)   (c)

5. Mateo **in May** **finished** business school. He **found** a job in July.
        (a)   (b)   (c)

6. I **visited** my hometown **recently**. **There was** a lot of new businesses.
     (a)   (b)   (c)

7. Marta **start** a successful business ten years ago, but she **sold** it **last year**.
         (a)   (b)   (c)

8. Their **technology** business **didn't employed** as many salespeople as **before**.
         (a)   (b)   (c)

2 Find and correct the mistakes in the paragraph about Rachael Ray.

Television personality Rachael Ray ~~grow~~ *grew* up around food. Her family owned several restaurants in Cape Cod, Massachusetts, and later her mother works as a food supervisor for some restaurants in upstate New York. Rachael also had several jobs in the food industry. One job was in a gourmet grocery store in Albany, New York. She noticed that people didn't bought many groceries because they didn't wanted to cook. They were working people, and there weren't enough time in their busy day for cooking. Rachael started cooking classes. In these classes, Rachael cooked meals in thirty minutes. The classes were very popular. She wrote in 1999 her first cookbook. There was many more cookbooks after that. The cookbooks were popular because the recipes were quick and easy to make. She in 2001 appeared on NBC's *Today Show*. The president of the Food Network sees Rachael and gave her a show on the network. She became a big star.

Self-Assessment

Circle the word or phrase that correctly completes each sentence.

1. What _____ to your brother's business?

   a. happen   b. happened   c. happens

2. I _____ any information about her business on Google.

   a. didn't find   b. didn't found   c. didn't finded

3. Last year, Anya _____ the Internet to sell her products.

   a. uses   b. used   c. use

4. _____ your parents _____ a successful business 20 years ago?

   a. Do . . . have   b. Did . . . had   c. Did . . . have

5. When _____ your business?

   a. you started   b. did you started   c. did you start

6. _____ government money to help finance our business last year.

   a. There is no   b. There was no   c. There were no

7. Oprah Winfrey _____ her own TV network in 2011.

   a. starts   b. start   c. started

8. Some famous entrepreneurs _____ to college.

   a. didn't go   b. didn't went   c. didn't

9. _____ Madam Walker a successful businesswoman?

   a. Were   b. Was   c. Did

10. _____ a problem with the new software program.

    a. There was   b. There were   c. There

11. _____ a new computer system for our business.

    a. We yesterday bought   b. We bought yesterday   c. Yesterday, we bought

12. _____ there many people at the meeting yesterday?

    a. Was   b. Is   c. Were

13. What _____ our last sales figures?

    a. were   b. was   c. was there

14. Julia and Ben _____ business degrees, but they were excellent salespeople.

    a. had not   b. didn't have   c. not have

15. He _____ 60,000 copies of his book *How to Start a Business*.

    a. sell   b. sold   c. selled

Simple Past, Time Clauses, *Used To*, and *Would*

Science and Society

Time Clauses and the Order of Past Events

1 Read the information about the steps that Teresa took to create an invention. Combine the sentences with time clauses. Do not use *then* or *immediately* in your answers. Add commas when necessary.

1. She chose a product that she used every day. Then she thought about ways to make it better.

   After *she chose a product that she used every day, she thought about ways to make it better* .

2. She thought of ideas. She wrote them down immediately.

   As soon as _____

   _____ .

3. She wrote about her idea. Then she talked to her friends.

   Before _____

   _____ .

4. She described her idea to friends. She immediately got feedback from them.

   When _____

   _____ .

5. She wrote the instructions for making her invention. Then she thought of a name for it.

   _____

   after _____ .

6. She searched for similar ideas on the Internet. Then she realized that her idea was unique.

   _____

   until _____ .

2 Read the paragraph about the Industrial Revolution. Write sentences with *after*, *before*, *when*, *as soon as*, and *until* and the simple past.

In the early 1800s, life changed a lot for people because there were many factories. This change, called the *Industrial Revolution*, started in the United Kingdom and spread throughout Europe, the United States, Canada, and later the rest of the world. For the first time, new machines made clothing and other products in these factories. Before that time, most people lived on farms. They made their own clothing and prepared their own food in traditional ways. However, with the invention of these machines, workers made products faster than before because they used different processes. People did not make their own things anymore. They bought products instead. After that, entrepreneurs built more factories and needed more people to work. People moved to the cities and worked in the factories. In that way, cities grew very quickly.

1. there / be / many factories   life / change / a lot for people

   (as soon as) _As soon as there were many factories, life changed a lot for people._

2. the Industrial Revolution   most people / live / on farms

   (until) _____

3. new machines / make / clothing / in factories   people / make / their own clothing

   (before) _____

4. people / invent / these machines   workers / make / products faster than before

   (after) _____

5. the factories / produce / the same goods   people / not make / their own things

   (as soon as) _____

6. entrepreneurs / build / more factories   they / need / more workers

   (as soon as) _____

7. people / move / to the cities   the cities / grow / quickly

   (when) _____

3 A Number the sentences in the correct order.

_1_ I just bought a new cell phone.

____ When my friends saw my new photo, they posted messages on my wall.

____ As soon as I got my phone connected and charged up, I took a photo of myself.

____ After I took my photo, I posted it on my favorite social networking site through my phone.

____ Until I got my new phone, I did not believe I could do all these things.

B Write sentences about something new that you bought. Use the sentences in A as a model.

1. Before I bought _my laptop, I had to go to the library a lot_ _____ .

2. As soon as I _____ .

3. When my friends _____ .

4. After I _____ .

5. Until I _____ .

Past with *Used To* and *Would*

1 Complete the blog. Use *used to* or *would* and the correct form of the verbs in parentheses. Sometimes more than one answer is possible.

Do you remember when people _used to write_ (write) letters on paper and send

(1)

them in the mail? My mother _____ (love) receiving letters. Times have

(2)

changed. My mom uses e-mail a lot more, and I mostly send e-mails and e-cards. My

grandmother _____ (live) on a farm when she was young. As a child, she

(3)

_____ (be) very excited when the mail came each day. She _____

(4)   (5)

often _____ (wait) for the mail carrier while reading a book. My life is so different

(5)

from hers. My grandmother remembers when computers _____ (be) a

(6)

luxury for many people. She also _____ (know) her friends' phone numbers

(7)

when she was my age. Because I have a cell phone, I can't remember my friends' phone

numbers – I just keep them in my phone. In the future, I will probably tell my children, "I

_____ (have) a laptop computer." I bet that they won't know what that is.

(8)

2 Complete the sentences about cameras. Use the simple past or *used to* with the verbs in parentheses. Sometimes more than one answer is possible.

Before

A Brownie camera

Now

A digital camera

1. When my grandmother was a child, she _used to have_ (have) a Brownie camera.

   She _____got_____ (get) the camera as a present on her tenth birthday.

2. She _____ (take) black-and-white pictures almost every day.

   She _____ (not / take) color pictures.

3. She _____ (wait) a long time to get the pictures developed.

   She _____ (not / see) the pictures immediately.

4. She _____ (sleep) with her Brownie camera.

   She _____ (love) it so much.

3 Answer questions with information that is true for you.

1. What inventions did you use to like when you were a child?

   _I used to like audio cassettes as a child._____

2. What things did you use to do when you were a child?

   _____

3. What would you do after school when you were bored?

   _____

4. What would you do on the weekends when you wanted some fun as a young teenager?

   _____

Avoid Common Mistakes

1 Circle the mistakes.

1. Miguel (use to) have an apartment before he **bought** his house.
   (a)   (b)   (c)

2. Where **did** she **used to** live before she **moved** to France?
         (a)   (b)   (c)

3. People **began** to **buy** ice cream as soon as **became** available.
           (a)   (b)   (c)

4. Jennifer **didn't used to** cook at home **until** her parents **gave** her a microwave oven.
             (a)   (b)   (c)

5. **After invented** the dishwasher, Josephine Cochrane **started** a company. Restaurants
   (a)   (b)
   bought the machine.
   (c)

6. We **use to** watch a small, old TV **until** we **bought** a new one.
        (a)   (b)   (c)

7. He continued to go to school **until** he **was** 18 years old. He **use to** study a lot.
                                 (a)   (b)   (c)

8. **After became** cheaper, more people **started** buying smart phones and **used** them all
   (a)   (b)   (c)
   the time.

2 Find and correct six more mistakes in the paragraph about the invention of the lightbulb.

How did people ~~used to~~ *use to* live before Thomas Edison invented the incandescent electric

lightbulb? For one thing, it wasn't very safe to travel after dark. When it got dark, businesses

use to close. People would use candles when needed light at home. However, candles

burned quickly, so people used them carefully. As a result, people didn't used to stay up late.

They went to bed soon after sundown. Before the lightbulb became popular, people use to

sleep 9 to 10 hours a night. After became more available, people only got around 6 hours of

sleep. Another change is that before electric lights, people didn't used to pay electric bills.

Now they do. Overall, electric lights are a very welcome and useful invention.

Self-Assessment

Circle the word or phrase that correctly completes each sentence.

1. Jill _____ a portable CD player. Now she has an MP4 player.

   a. would have   b. has   c. used to have

2. _____ we had a clothes dryer, we would hang our clothes outside to dry.

   a. As soon as   b. Until   c. After

3. My grandparents _____ travel very often. Now they love to travel on airplanes.

   a. didn't used to   b. use to   c. didn't use to

4. Before cell phones, how _____ you make a phone call?

   a. would   b. wouldn't   c. used to

5. People would usually walk to work _____ public transportation was available.

   a. as soon as   b. after   c. before

6. When electric refrigerators became available, people _____ blocks of ice.

   a. didn't used to need   b. didn't need   c. didn't use to need

7. Dora _____ much television, but now she watches it all day long.

   a. didn't used to watch   b. use to watch   c. didn't use to watch

8. It was difficult to move products across the United States _____ railroads existed.

   a. before   b. when   c. as soon as

9. How did we _____ our lives before computers?

   a. used to   b. use to manage   c. used to manage

10. Before e-mail, I _____ mostly communicate with my friends by phone.

    a. wouldn't   b. would   c. use to

11. Susan never used to take a lot of pictures until she _____ her digital camera.

    a. bought   b. would buy   c. used to buy

12. Buses were often uncomfortable in summer _____ they had air conditioning.

    a. when   b. after   c. until

13. Before there were highways in the United States, _____ many weeks to travel across the country.

    a. it would take   b. use to take   c. took

14. It _____ more dangerous to drive. Now we have seat belts in our cars.

    a. use to be   b. used to be   c. didn't used to bc

15. _____ scientists discovered vitamins, we learned how to eat healthier.

    a. Before   b. When   c. Until

Past Progressive

Memorable Events

Past Progressive

1 Complete the paragraphs about the 2008 U.S. Presidential election. Use the past progressive form of the verbs in parentheses.

On November 4, 2008, the people of the United States _were waiting_ (wait) to
(1)

learn the name of their next president. John McCain and Barack Obama were the

two candidates. On that evening, people _____ (gather)
(2)

in two U.S. cities to hear special speeches from each candidate. One group

_____ (form) outside a big hotel in Phoenix, Arizona. These
(3)

people _____ (hope) to hear a victory speech by John
(4)

McCain. Obama supporters _____ (meet) at Grant Park in
(5)

Chicago, Illinois. They _____ (expect) a victory speech from
(6)

Barack Obama.

Late at night, the news finally reported the results. Obama was the winner.

The response from Obama's supporters in Chicago was loud and clear. They

_____ (cheer) for a long time. At the same time, McCain
(7)

_____ (give) a speech to announce his loss and to wish Obama
(8)

good luck.

2 Read the conversation about the blizzard of 1991 in Minneapolis. Complete the questions and answers with the past progressive form of the verbs in parentheses.

A: _Were you living_ (you / live) in Minneapolis, Minnesota, in 1991? I heard that 28
        (1)

inches of snow fell over two days.

B: Yes, _I was living_ (I / live) there at the time with my family. It was a memorable day
         (2)

because it was also Halloween.

A: _____ (what / you / do) on that day?
        (3)

B: Well, I was 8 years old. _____ (I / not feel) well, so I was home,
        (4)

but my brothers were at school. _____
        (5)

(my mom / not work), so she was home, too. _____
        (6)

(my dad / drive) a taxi.

A: _____ (it / snow) hard?
        (7)

B: _____ (the snow / not come) down hard
        (8)

at first. But by lunchtime, _____ (the wind / blow), too.
        (9)

I remember walking into the kitchen and seeing my mom. _____
        (10)

(she / watch) the weather reports on TV. The reports showed images of the snow all

over the city. My mom looked very worried. I know that _____
        (11)

(she / think) about my dad.

A: Did anyone go trick-or-treating that night?

B: Not many, but my brothers did. They said that _____ (people / give)
        (12)

them lots of candy because no one else was out.

3 Complete the sentences about a strange event at Niagara Falls. Circle the correct prepositions. Then write the past progressive form of the verbs in parentheses.

1. **On**/ **At** March 29, 1848, a local farmer ___*was walking*___ (walk) near Niagara Falls at night.

2. **At / On** midnight, he noticed that the water _____ (flow) very slowly.

3. **In / At** 7:30 the next morning, people _____ (report) that Niagara Falls was dry. Everyone was shocked.

4. **In / On** that day, some people thought the world _____ (come) to an end. Nobody could believe the story!

5. **In / At** the afternoon, Niagara Falls was full of people. They _____ (wander) around and _____ (look) for souvenirs.

6. The falls did not stop for long. **On / In** March 31, the water _____ (fall) again.

4 Write answers to the questions that are true for you. Use the past progressive.

1. What were you doing in the summer of 2011?

   In the summer of 2011, I was working at an ice cream store.

2. Who were you spending a lot of time with?

   _____

3. How were you feeling?

   _____

4. What were you thinking about?

   _____

Using *When* and *While* with Past Progressive

1 Complete the sentences about a World Cup soccer game. Use the simple past or past progressive form of the verbs in the boxes.

be	give	~~go~~	have	see	wait

My father and I _went_ to a World Cup soccer game last year. We _____
(1)   (2)

in line to buy tickets when my dad _____ a friend of his. His friend
(3)

_____ two extra tickets. He _____ them to my dad. My dad
(4)   (5)

_____ so happy.
(6)

be	begin	jump	practice	run	sit	spill

The teams _____ already _____ on the field
(7)   (7)

when we _____ down. Our seats _____ right at
(8)   (9)

the midfield line. It was great! At 1:00, the game _____ . While our
(10)

favorite player _____ down the field with the ball, the man behind me
(11)

_____ up and _____ his drink all over me.
(12)   (13)

2 Combine the sentences about the 2003 blackout in New York City using the simple past and past progressive.

1. People stood on a subway platform.

   The power went out.

   While _people were standing on a subway_
   platform, _the power went out_ .

2. People called for help on their cell phones.

   Two police officers arrived with flashlights.

   _____

   when _____ .

3. One police officer led people to a stairway.

   The other officer tried to calm people down.

   _____

   while _____.

4. People walked to the stairway.

   They helped each other.

   While _____,

   _____.

5. Outside, people talked and called friends on their cell phones.

   A restaurant worker came and brought them cold bottles of water.

   _____

   when _____.

3 Read the conversations about memorable events. Write questions with the past progressive and the simple past.

1. What / they / do / when / her husband / propose?

   Q: _What were they doing when her husband proposed?_

   A: They were eating dinner.

2. What / you / think about / when / you / come to / America?

   Q: _____

   A: I was thinking about how nervous I was!

3. Where / you / go / when / you / see / the movie star?

   Q: _____

   A: I was going to the movie theater with some friends.

4. Who / you / visit / when / the blizzard / start?

   Q: _____

   A: I was visiting my brother in Canada. It was so cold!

5. What / she / hear / while / she / watch / TV?

   Q: _____

   A: She heard the results of the election.

6. He / text / while / the president / speak?

   Q: _____

   A: Yes, he was. He was telling his mom that he saw the president.

Avoid Common Mistakes

1 Circle the mistakes.

1. My first day at school **was** memorable. I **were going** to Springhill School. I **was** six years old.
   (a)   (b)   (c)

2. Where **the millennium celebration was taking** place? Where **were people gathering**?
              (a)   (b)

   Where **were they watching** fireworks?
              (c)

3. We stayed home while it **was raining**. Tom had an accident while he **drove** in the rain.
                                (a)   (b)

   While the rain **was falling**, we watched television indoors.
                        (c)

4. **When Dave graduated,** we had a party. **When he got a job,** we had another party.
          (a)   (b)

   When he got married. We had the best party.
          (c)

5. **When we went to Florida** we watched a rocket take off. **When it went up,** fire was
          (a)   (b)

   coming out at the bottom. **While it was flying away,** it looked very small.
                                    (c)

6. When I went downtown, a crowd **was standing** on the sidewalk. While I **were trying** to find
                                        (a)   (b)

   out why, someone said, "The president is here." When I saw the president, I **was** amazed.
                                                                                        (c)

7. Why **were you standing** on the sidewalk yesterday? Who **you were trying** to see?
            (a)   (b)

   What **was happening** there?
              (c)

8. **When the storm started,** I was brushing my teeth. **When lightning was flashing,** I got
          (a)   (b)

   scared. **While the wind was blowing.** The lights went out.
                    (c)

2 Find and correct the mistakes in the article about a space shuttle.

The Last U.S. Shuttle Flight

On July 21, 2011, Duane and Emma Wilson ~~was~~ *were* sitting in front of the television in their home in Dallas, Texas. What they were watching? The space shuttle Atlantis were coming back to Earth after 12 days in space. While the Wilsons watched TV, Atlantis was landing in Florida. Other people was watching from the ground in Florida. Why were so many people watching? Atlantis was the last U.S. space shuttle. When the shuttle landed people were talking about the end of the space flight program. People was celebrating the shuttle's return, but they were also sad. This wasn't the end of space exploration, though. NASA was already making plans to travel to Mars. When Atlantis landed.

Self-Assessment

Circle the word or phrase that correctly completes each sentence.

1. Who _____ next to at the party last night?

   a. was you sitting   b. were you sitting   c. you were sitting

2. _____ the Fourth of July, we were watching fireworks.

   a. In   b. At   c. On

3. Last May, someone tried to rob Sam's house. He and his wife _____ when their security alarm went off.

   a. sleeping   b. slept   c. were sleeping

4. Jeff and Rachel had tickets to a concert. They were getting dressed for the concert _____ the babysitter arrived.

   a. while   b. when   c. , while

5. Lisa and I _____ where you were when astronauts first reached the moon.

   a. were wondering   b. was wondering   c. wondering

6. Pat was visiting her family in Chile when she _____ the flu.

   a. was getting   b. was got   c. got

7. While I was walking through the mall, a man _____ me a flyer that said, "You won a prize!"

   a. gave   b. was giving   c. was gave

8. Where _____ when the new millennium started in 2000?

   a. you were living   b. were you living   c. you living

9. _____ November 19, 1863, Abraham Lincoln was giving a famous speech in Gettysburg, Pennsylvania.

   a. In   b. On   c. At

10. Thousands of people _____ on the streets of New York City when World War II ended.

    a. was celebrating   b. were celebrating   c. was

11. While a satellite was exploring the moon in 2009, it _____ water.

    a. discovered   b. discover   c. was discovering

12. We _____ home when we heard about the election.

    a. were driving   b. were drive   c. driving

13. What were you studying _____ ?

    a. in year   b. last year   c. on year

14. **A:** Was Brian taking a trip around the world last year? **B:** _____ .

    a. No, he didn't   b. Yes, he was   c. No, he weren't

15. I shook hands with the president _____ around the country in 2011.

    a. when he was traveling   b. , when he was traveling   c. , when he traveled

Count and Noncount Nouns

Privacy Matters

Count Nouns and Noncount Nouns

1 Write the nouns in the box in the correct columns. Then write the plural forms of the count nouns.

account	bill	computer	help	number	privacy	site	trust
advice	card	garbage	information	page	respect	software	work

Noncount Nouns					
1.	*advice*	4.		7.	
2.		5.		8.	
3.		6.		9.	

Count Nouns	
Singular Form	**Plural Form**
1. *account*	*accounts*
2.	
3.	
4.	
5.	
6.	
7.	

2 Read the posts from an online chat room. Circle the correct words.

mom38inla:	I need (some help)/ a help. My daughter spends most of her (1) time alone in her room. I was starting to worry about her. I found her cell phone and read some text **message / messages** from (2) her friends. She found out and got very angry. Does anyone have **suggestion / a suggestion** for me about what to do? (3)
tomtsmiley:	**My son / Son** is angry with me for the same reason. He has (4) **a computer / some computer** in his bedroom. I knew he went to (5) a lot of **website / websites**, but I didn't know which ones. I worry (6) about the security of the websites, so I checked his computer to find out where he goes. He got really angry with me.
sandylee5:	Young people need **privacy / privacies**. **My advice / An advice** (7) (8) is to tell your kids that you trust them and that you'll respect their privacy, but give them rules to follow.

3 Complete the sentences about shopping online. Use the singular or plural form of the nouns in parentheses. Add *a* or *an* when necessary. Then check (✓) the boxes to show whether the nouns are count (C) or noncount (NC).

1. I bought two shirts online. I had _*a bad experience*_ (bad experience). ☑ C ☐ NC

2. I had to set up _____ (account) with the company. ☐ C ☐ NC

3. The company asked a lot of _____ (question) about me. ☐ C ☐ NC

4. I paid with _____ (credit card) on their site. ☐ C ☐ NC

5. I didn't think that the site was unsafe. I made _____ (big mistake). ☐ C ☐ NC

6. The next day, someone used my card to buy some _____ (furniture). ☐ C ☐ NC

7. I didn't worry about _____ (security) that day, but now I do. ☐ C ☐ NC

8. I didn't know the company. I was not careful about online _____ (safety). ☐ C ☐ NC

Noncount Nouns: Determiners and Measurement Words

1 Complete the conversation about cell phone privacy. Circle the correct words.

Heather: I heard **an** /**(some)** interesting information the other day. Cell phone companies
(1)

are aware of your location.

Kevin: Really? I guess there isn't **any / some** privacy anymore.
(2)

Heather: I guess not. Actually, cell phone companies get **a lot of / many** information
(3)

about their customers.

Kevin: I had no idea.

Heather: **Many / Much** people don't know about it.
(4)

Kevin: I'm a bit concerned about that.

Heather: In some ways, it's good. When the police don't have **too much / enough**
(5)

evidence about a crime, they can request the phone records of a

suspected criminal.

Kevin: Amazing! I don't see **some / any** problem with that.
(6)

Heather: I agree, but I heard **a piece of / a** news the other day that concerned me. Cell
(7)

phone companies can track the location of any phone that has GPS.

Kevin: Wow! Do **a lot of / much** phones have GPS?
(8)

Heather: Yes, **many / much** phones do. Luckily, cell phone companies can't sell this
(9)

information, though.

Kevin: So, what **an / piece of** advice can you give me to protect my privacy?
(10)

Heather: Well, you can turn off **some / any** features on your phone – like GPS.
(11)

Kevin: That's **good / a good** idea. I don't use my GPS anyway.
(12)

Heather: You can also delete **a few / some** sensitive information – such as phone
(13)

numbers or text messages.

Kevin: Thanks for **your / an** advice, Heather!
(14)

2 Complete the lists with the correct measurement words in the boxes. Some measurement
words are plural. Add *a* when necessary.

LIST A

bowl of	cup of	~~glass of~~	packet of	piece of

What I Like for Breakfast

1. _____*a glass of*_____ juice

2. two _____ hot coffee with two _____ sugar

3. two _____ toast

4. _____ cereal

LIST B

bag of	bar of	box of	can of	gallon of	loaf of	pound of	tube of

Shopping List

1. _____ rice

2. _____ milk

3. two _____ soap

4. _____ butter

5. two _____ bread

6. two _____ soup

7. _____ cereal

8. _____ toothpaste

3 Answer the questions about privacy. Write sentences that are true for you. Use one of the words or phrases in parentheses.

1. How much privacy do you have at work or at school? (enough / don't . . . much)

   I have enough privacy at school. OR *I don't have much privacy at work.*

2. How much time do you spend on the Internet at work or at school? (a lot of / don't . . . much)

   _____

3. How much time do you spend on social networking sites? (too much / a little)

   _____

4. How much control does your boss or your college have over your Internet use? (some / a lot of)

   _____

5. How many personal phone calls do you think people should make at work? (a few / not . . . many)

   _____

Avoid Common Mistakes

1 Circle the mistakes.

1. Don't give your e-mail **address** to too many companies. A company can sell (**address**) to
   (a)   (b)
   someone. You will get too many e-mail **messages**.
                                              (c)

2. I keep **an information** about myself private. I don't give **credit card information** to
          (a)   (b)
   anyone. I don't go to **any social networking sites**.
                          (c)

3. Choose good **passwords** for your accounts. Use **numbers and letters**. That will
                  (a)   (b)
   increase your **safeties**.
                  (c)

4. Body scanners provide **security** in airports. However, there are **not enough scanners**
                           (a)   (b)
   for all airports. The government is not making **many progress** in providing them.
                                                   (c)

5. **Some ID thieves** go through your garbage. They can get **much information** about
      (a)   (b)
   you from the documents that you throw away. **A lot of online thieves** get personal
                                                 (c)
   information with phishing e-mails.

6. I bought **a new security program** for my computer. It can find **virus** in an e-mail. It
              (a)   (b)
   also can find **spyware**.
                  (c)

7. I gave **a permission** for my friend to use my computer. However, I do not let him see
   (a)

   any e-mail messages in my account. I have **a password** that protects my privacy.
   (b)   (c)

8. A cell phone company knows all about a customer's **calls**. It can also do **research**
                                                        (a)   (b)

   to know where a customer usually goes. Cell phone companies have too much

   informations about us.
   (c)

2 Find and correct eight more mistakes in the web article about student privacy.

Law Protects Students' Privacy

In 1974, ⏺the⏺ U.S. government passed the Family Educational Rights and Privacy

Act (FERPA). This is law that protects the privacies of students. The law explains

what details schools can give about students. The FERPA law says that there

are two kinds of an information about students – "directory information" and

"non-directory information." "Directory information" includes facts such as your

name, your address, your phone number, and your major. Schools can share

these things about student without a permission. As a result, people can learn

much information about you. Some students worry that this could threaten

their securities. If you don't want your school to give "directory" details about

you, you can ask the school not to share many knowledge they have about you.

"Non-directory information" includes things such as your social security number,

your student identification number, your grades, and details about your schedule.

Schools can't give this information without permission.

Self-Assessment

Circle the word or phrase that correctly completes each sentence.

1. Some websites share your information without _____ .

   a. a permission   b. permissions   c. your permission

2. Brian ordered three _____ while he was at the café.

   a. cup of coffee   b. coffee   c. cups of coffee

3. New _____ more security to protect computers from spyware.

   a. software provides   b. softwares provide   c. software provide

4. With phishing e-mails, some criminals got _____ about David's bank account.

   a. much information   b. some informations   c. a lot of information

5. Travelers don't have _____ privacy in airports. Scanners get very personal information.

   a. a few   b. enough   c. too many

6. The police didn't have _____ against the man who stole my identity.

   a. too much evidences   b. many evidence   c. any evidence

7. If you block _____ , you have more privacy on the Internet.

   a. cookie   b. a cookies   c. cookies

8. Some websites record your online research. Then they send you _____ advertising about topics that you searched for.

   a. a lot of   b. an   c. any

9. Eric spends _____ on the Internet and not enough time studying.

   a. too many times   b. too much time   c. any time

10. I think online banking is dangerous. There are _____ for ID thieves to get your account information.

    a. too many ways   b. too much way   c. too ways

11. Javier didn't make _____ on his research paper because spyware made his computer crash.

    a. not much progress   b. many progress   c. much progress

12. I bought a _____ expensive soap online, and the company stole my credit card number.

    a. slice of   b. bar of   c. sheet of

13. To protect _____ , there are body scanners in U.S. airports.

    a. traveler   b. a travelers   c. travelers

14. Social networking sites are fun, but don't give away _____ information about yourself.

    a. some   b. much   c. many

15. _____ is, "Don't give any information that the whole world shouldn't know."

    a. Good advices   b. Some good advice   c. A few advice

UNIT 8

Articles
The Media

Articles

1 Complete the paragraph about a tsunami in Indonesia. Circle the correct articles.

On December 26, 2004, **a** / **the** terrible natural
(1)
disaster struck **an** / **the** coast of northern
(2)
Sumatra, in Indonesia. **A** / **An** huge wave, called
(3)
a *tsunami*, washed over **the** / **a** cities and towns.
(4)
It destroyed telephone lines, electrical systems,
and almost all of northern Sumatra's links to
a / **the** world. "Citizen journalists" shared the
(5)

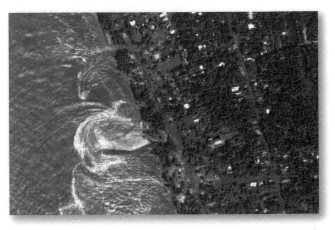

range of destruction with the world through social networking sites and blogs. **The** / **A** citizen
(6)
journalist is an ordinary person who uses photos, blogs, wikis, and video-sharing sites to record

events. Because phone service in some areas was still working, **a** / **the** citizen journalists sent
(7)
a / **the** pictures and reports to **an** / **the** Indonesian government and other organizations that
(8)   (9)
could help. Reporters from traditional news media like television and newspapers could not

reach **an** / **the** area for many days. During that time, citizen journalists provided the only
(10)
reports about **a** / **the** disaster.
(11)

2 Read about citizen journalism. Complete the sentences with *a / an*, *the*, or Ø for no article.
Sometimes more than one answer is possible.

1. Citizen journalism has become __*an*__ important source of news.

2. _____ citizen journalist is not _____ professional. He or she did not go to
journalism school.

3. This type of journalist provides _____ information about current events. This person

acts like _____ reporter. Citizen journalists sometimes analyze events, too.

4. Citizen journalists report _____ news of the day differently.

5. Some citizen journalists use _____ blogs. Some post their videos on _____ video-sharing site, such as YouTube.

6. These journalists also post them on _____ social networking sites.

7. Some citizen journalists take _____ pictures using their cell phones and post them online.

8. Some of _____ news stories on TV are also from citizen journalists.

9. Some people criticize citizen journalists. They believe that all reporters should have _____ good education in journalism.

10. Recently, _____ article on citizen journalism discussed the importance of this type of journalism. _____ article also included some important citizen-journalism websites.

3 Unscramble the sentences about the media today. Use the correct form of the verbs. Add *the* before the nouns in bold when appropriate.

whitehouse.gov

1. be / whitehouse.gov / **government's** official website

   Whitehouse.gov is the government's official website.

2. can / send / anyone / **president** / an e-mail from this site

   _____

3. sign up / for tours / **public** / can also

   _____

4. come to the site to listen to / **press** / every day / statements about current events

   _____

weather.gov

5. anywhere in **country** / provides information / weather.gov / about **weather**

   _____

6. to the media / it / provides **information**

   _____

nasa.gov

7. have / nasa.gov / information about space exploration now and in **past**

   _____

8. you / at nasa.gov / can see / pictures of **moon, sun**, and **universe**

   _____

9. of places / nasa.gov / show / images / around **world**

   _____

Generalizing: More About Articles

1 Rewrite the statements about the media. Make the singular nouns in bold plural. Make the plural nouns in bold singular. Change the articles and verbs when necessary.

1. A **blog** is an online **journal** or **report**.

   Blogs are online journals or reports.

2. Company **blogs** tell **consumers** what is happening with **companies**.

   A company blog tells a consumer what is happening with a company.

3. News **blogs** comment on the news of the day.

   _____

4. **Tweets** are **posts** on Twitter.

   _____

5. A **podcast** is a convenient way to hear a news **story**.

   _____

6. A media **app** is an **app** that gives you the news on your electronic **device**.

   _____

7. **People** download **podcasts** on digital **players** or **computers**.

   _____

8. Educational **blogs** are **blogs** that **teachers** use.

   _____

2 Complete the statements about very young media users. Use *a*, *the*, or Ø for no article. Add capital letters when necessary.

1. _A_ toddler is _a_ child who is from one to three years of age.

2. Studies show that _____ toddlers who watch a lot of TV exercise less.

3. Some pediatricians say that _____ child under two should not watch TV.

4. _____ preschoolers are children who are from three to five years of age.

5. _____ preschooler often watches about two hours of TV every day.

6. Most children have _____ computer at home.

7. The age that _____ child begins playing games on the Web is around six years old.

8. _____ study showed that _____ young boys are more interested in video games than _____ young girls.

9. Almost 30 percent of children live in _____ homes where the TV is on most of the time.

10. _____ children who did not watch TV had better reading abilities than those who watched TV.

3 Complete the sentences about media use. Write sentences that are true for you.

1. Most teens _watch too much TV on their computers_____ .

2. A lot of adults _____ .

3. Some students _____ .

4. Some young children _____ .

Avoid Common Mistakes

1 Circle the mistakes.

1. Ø News websites sent Rob (message) about an important news story.
   (a)   (b)   (c)

2. **The** editors at newspapers often use **the** Internet to look up Ø information.
   (a)   (b)   (c)

3. Will Ø consumers get more news from Ø Internet or **the** radio in the next 10 years?
        (a)   (b)   (c)

4. Ø movie stars usually don't have **the** privacy because **the** press watches everything they do.
   (a)   (b)   (c)

5. **A lot of** advertisements cost Ø companies **the** money.
   (a)   (b)   (c)

6. Sometimes you can get **the** good advice from **the** comments on Ø websites.
                        (a)   (b)   (c)

7. **Some** people want **the** media to do more stories on Ø environment.
   (a)   (b)   (c)

8. Jessica is saving Ø money for Ø new cell phone with Ø modern technology.
   (a)   (b)   (c)

2 Find and correct the mistakes in the web article about podcasts.

article   discussion   podcast

Podcasts

people
These days, ~~the people~~ are getting the news in new ways. A lot of people read blogs, but now they can also listen to the news or watch it on their digital devices. They can also subscribe to get podcasts. Podcast is a sound file. The users download podcasts from websites on Internet. When you go to a website, you sometimes see download button. If you click on download button, you can download the podcast. Then you can listen to podcast on a computer or other digital devices. Podcasts are often free. Then the website automatically downloads podcast to a program, such as iTunes. Podcasts give the information on many different topics, including sports, environment, the entertainment, politics, and the health.

Self-Assessment

Circle the word or phrase that correctly completes each sentence.

1. Does _____ government own the media in this country?

   a. Ø   b. the   c. a

2. _____ television channel that I always watch at 6:00 p.m. has a news show.

   a. A   b. Ø   c. The

3. _____ headline is a title for a news story.

   a. A   b. The   c. Ø

4. Many people get the news from _____ Internet.

   a. an   b. a   c. the

5. Some parts of _____ world do not have any connection to the Internet.

   a. the   b. a   c. Ø

6. Yu-Man watched a show on television last night. _____ show was about new technology.

   a. A   b. The   c. An

7. Melissa is interested in hearing more about _____ environment on the news.

   a. an   b. Ø   c. the

8. _____ information is any fact or statement that adds to your knowledge.

   a. An   b. Ø   c. The

9. New technology leads to _____ new forms of media.

   a. Ø   b. the   c. a

10. Companies that advertise on _____ websites can count the people who read their ads.

    a. the   b. Ø   c. a

11. _____ teenagers use the Internet for research, but many also use it to communicate with friends.

    a. The   b. A   c. A lot of

12. I watched a great video online, but I can't remember _____ title of it.

    a. the   b. a   c. Ø

13. Ordinary people can report the news with _____ cell phones and the Internet.

    a. a   b. Ø   c. the

14. A good blogger can create a lot of publicity for _____ new product.

    a. Ø   b. a   c. the

15. People can read _____ books on computers, but many people still prefer to have paper books.

    a. the   b. a   c. Ø

Pronouns; Direct and Indirect Objects

Challenging Ourselves

Pronouns

1 Complete the chart. Write the missing pronouns.

Subject Pronoun	Object Pronoun	Possessive Determiner	Possessive Pronoun	Reflexive Pronoun
I	me	my	*mine*	
you	you			
he		his		
she				herself
it		its	————	
we	us		ours	
they				themselves

2 Complete the paragraphs about courageous people. Circle the correct pronouns.

A Erik Weihenmayer can't see. He lost **him / (his)** eyesight when he was 13. However,

(1)

on May 25, 2001, **him / he** became the first blind man to climb Mount Everest. **He / It**

(2) (3)

is the highest mountain in the world. After **him / his** successful climb, a school for

(4)

blind students in Tibet asked **he / him** for help. They wanted to be mountain climbers,

(5)

too. Eric taught **their / them** how to climb. The students worked hard. **Their / They**

(6) (7)

climbed Mount Everest. They climbed almost to the top of **it / its**. The students were

(8)

very proud of **their / themselves**.

(9)

B J. K. Rowling, the writer of the *Harry Potter* novels, also had some difficult challenges in her life. After a divorce, **she / her** moved from Portugal to Edinburgh, Scotland.
(10)

She wanted to be near **his / her** sister. She took care of her
(11)
daughter by **her / herself**. Her job did not pay much, so she
(12)
and her daughter had to live on about $100 a week from the government. In an interview, J. K. Rowling said, "**I / Me** was
(13)
very angry at **me / myself**. I did not want to be in that
(14)
situation." However, she never stopped trying to reach

her / hers goal of writing a novel. She finished writing the first *Harry Potter* novel in 1995, and she
(15)
was a millionaire five years later.

3 Complete the sentences about achieving goals. Use possessive and reflexive pronouns.

1. I talked to successful people I know. Many of them said that they became successful because they
   believed in ___*themselves*___ .

2. My brother and sister have achieved their dreams. He has a small business, and she is a teacher.
   His dream was to be his own boss, and _____ was to teach children.

3. My brother says that successful people tell _____ that they can achieve their dreams.

4. My sister says that she imagined _____ as a teacher.

5. My friend José and I have different goals. His goal is different from _____ .

6. My goal is to own a house. _____ is to have a well-paid accounting job.

7. My friends and I push _____ in our classes, and we try hard.

8. My family and I all have different dreams. We all have different dreams from _____ .

4 Complete the conversations with *one* or *ones*.

1. **A:** Look at these two bike races – 20 miles and 40 miles. Which <u>one</u> do you prefer?

   B: I like the 20-mile race. It's shorter.

2. **A:** Which yoga classes do you take?

   B: I take two. I take the _____ on Tuesday and Thursday mornings.

3. **A:** Look at these two pairs of hiking boots. I don't know which _____ to buy.

   B: The dark brown boots are nicer.

   A: I don't know. I think the tan _____ are better.

4. **A:** Which gym should I join?

   B: The gym on Elm Street is open until 10:00 p.m. The _____ on Main Street is not very expensive.

5. **A:** We're saving as much money as possible this year. Do you know a good bank?

   B: The _____ near my house has free checking and savings accounts.

   A: Great. I'll go there.

5 Complete the sentences with the correct reciprocal or reflexive pronouns.

1. My sister Kate and I went to a workshop on nursing at our school. Before we arrived, we promised <u>*each other*</u> that we would not be shy.

2. I introduced <u>*myself*</u> to the presenter. My sister also introduced _____ to the presenter. We introduced _____ .

3. I met a really interesting woman. We talked to _____ for a long time.

4. Kate wanted to talk to a guy who was in one of her classes, but she was afraid. I said, "Kate, challenge _____ . You can do it. Say hello."

5. Kate and the guy smiled at _____ .

6. Then Kate and the guy walked over to _____ and introduced _____ .

7. Kate and the guy asked _____ questions about their lives.

8. They decided to meet _____ after class to talk about the homework.

9. My sister challenged _____ , and now she and the guy from the class are married!

Direct and Indirect Objects

1 Circle the direct object and underline the indirect object in each sentence.

1. The school gave the soccer team an award.

2. The coach told the team the good news.

3. The school gave the team a check to buy new equipment.

4. The team showed their new equipment to the crowd at the next game.

5. The parents gave a party for the team.

2 Read the paragraph about improving Paul's performance at work. Complete the sentences with *for*, *to*, or X for no preposition.

Paul was doing badly at work. He wanted to improve his performance at work, so he asked his best friend __*for*__ advice. His best friend was very successful at his job. His best
(1)

friend e-mailed ___X___ him some helpful websites. He also made _____ him a
(2)   (3)

list of ideas and tasks. At his job, Paul asked _____ his co-workers _____ advice.
(4)   (5)

His co-workers told _____ him to listen more carefully at meetings. One co-worker
(6)

showed _____ her "to do" lists _____ him. She also offered to help _____
(7)   (8)   (9)

him write "to do" lists each morning. His supervisor e-mailed some articles on time

management _____ him. Paul worked hard. Six months later, his supervisor offered
(10)

_____ him a promotion.
(11)

3 Diana and Jeff decided to move to a new city. Below are their "to do" lists one month before they left. Answer the questions on the next page. Write the sentences two ways: In the first sentence, use prep + IO (noun). In the second sentence, put the IO before the DO, and use a pronoun for the IO.

Diana's "To Do" List	Jeff's "To Do" List
Sarah – buy a present	Landlord – pay rent
Tina – give clothes	All my friends – send e-mail with new address
Paul – give textbooks	Ben – offer video game console
All my friends – send invitations to going-away party	Ivan – sell car

1. What did Diana buy Sarah?

   Diana bought a present for Sarah.

   Diana bought her a present.

2. What did Diana send to her friends?

3. What did Jeff pay the landlord?

4. Who gave textbooks to Paul?

5. What did Jeff sell to Ivan?

6. Who did Diana give clothes to?

7. What did Jeff send his friends?

8. What did Jeff offer to Ben?

4 Think about a challenge you had at some time in your life. Answer the questions about the challenge. Use pronouns and prepositions when possible. Circle the pronouns and underline the prepositions.

1. What was the challenge?

   (It) was asking my teacher for advice.

2. What did you do?

3. Who offered you help?

4. Who gave you good advice?

5. What was the result of the challenge?

Avoid Common Mistakes

1 Circle the mistakes.

1. I gave a challenge to **Rosa and Miguel**. I told (he and she), "Run a mile." **They** love to run.
   (a)   (b)   (c)

2. I offered **to him my help**. I said I could lend **my tools to him**. I gave **him my address**.
   (a)   (b)   (c)

3. The college is giving a challenge **for us**. We need to get top grades in all **our** courses.
   (a)   (b)

   Then they will give free books **to us**.
   (c)

4. My grandfather bought my **sister a special book**. He bought **her his favorite book**
   (a)   (b)

   from his childhood. He gave **her it**.
   (c)

5. Did **you** challenge **to her** to a game of chess? Did you give **me** the same challenge?
   (a)   (b)   (c)

6. Maria wants to give a good life **to her family**. She bought a piano **to her son** and a new
   (a)   (b)

   laptop **for her daughter**.
   (c)

7. Tom needs a bike **for his race**. I can't **lend him it**. Can you lend **your bike to him**?
   (a)   (b)   (c)

8. Theresa told one story to **them**. She told another one to **you and I**. She told a different
   (a)   (b)

   story to **him and her**.
   (c)

2 Find and correct nine more mistakes in this article about learning another language.

The Challenge of a New Language

    Six years ago, Marta Ortiz moved from Guatemala to the United States with her children. ~~Her~~ *She*

and her children did not speak very much English, so life was hard at first. Soon the children started

school and them made friends. When they did not know a word, their friends taught them it. They

learned quickly. At work, Marta's co-workers spoke Spanish, so it was a challenge to learn English.

When her children brought home a letter from school, they would read her it. Sometimes Marta

needed to make a phone call in English. Her son did it to she. The children wanted to help she. They

made for themselves dinner so that their mother could take an English class in the evenings. Marta

liked her classmates. She liked to speak English, and she started to learn. Now Marta is taking an

advanced English class. Her teacher gives to her good grades. He gives advice for her about colleges.

Her daughter and son are very proud. Soon her English will be as good as theirs.

Self-Assessment

Circle the word or phrase that correctly completes each sentence.

1. Yi-Yin's grandfather never went to school. He taught _____ to read.

    a. itself   b. himself   c. him

2. Kelly's exercise class is near her job. _____ is in my building.

    a. I   b. Me   c. Mine

3. _____ are taking a Chinese class. It's really challenging.

    a. Me and my friends   b. My friends and myself   c. My friends and I

4. She is learning how to fix computers. I didn't need my old one, so I gave _____ .

    a. her it   b. it to her   c. it her

5. My aunt and uncle can't drive themselves to the doctor, so I drive _____ .

    a. them   b. they   c. one another

6. Jake's apartment is too small for his family. He's looking for a bigger _____ .

    a. ones   b. one   c. it

7. Sam and Mona like to go out, but it's difficult. Their children are too young to stay _____ .

    a. themselves   b. by herself   c. by themselves

8. You need to challenge yourself if you want to reach _____ .

    a. you goals   b. your goals   c. yours goals

9. Dmitry always volunteers to help other people. He doesn't usually think about _____ .

    a. him   b. himself   c. he

10. Adam's mother was in the hospital last week. He sent _____ .

    a. her some flowers   b. to her some flowers   c. some flowers her

11. Wendy and Hong have a strong friendship. They always help _____ in difficult times.

    a. them   b. ones   c. each other

12. Our friend lost her wedding ring. She had pictures of it, so she showed _____ .

    a. them for us   b. us them   c. them to us

13. Amanda thinks she can win the speaking competition. She practiced by _____ .

    a. herself   b. himself   c. itself

14. After we finished our project, we helped them finish _____ .

    a. theirs project   b. theirs   c. their

15. Ed has great stories about life's challenges. In his stories, people often help _____ .

    a. them   b. one   c. each other

Present Perfect

Discoveries

Present Perfect

1 Complete the paragraphs about space. Use the present perfect form of the verbs in the boxes.

ask	build	collect	~~look~~	send

For thousands of years, people *have looked* up at the sky at night.
                                        (1)

Many people _____ , "Is there life on other planets?"
                        (2)

Scientists _____ telescopes to look deep into space. They
                    (3)

_____ information about the moon, Venus, Mars, Jupiter, Saturn,
            (4)

and other planets. Our government _____ satellites into space to
                                            (5)

learn more about the universe.

decide	find	identify	learn	send	start	study

Researchers _____ a lot from the telescopes and satellites.
                        (6)

For example, some scientists _____ evidence of water on
                                    (7)

the moon. Also, a robot _____ pictures from Mars. Scientists
                                (8)

_____ these pictures. They _____ that there
            (9)   (10)

probably is water on Mars, too. Now we _____ to look deeper into
                                                (11)

space. Researchers _____ over 460 planets that may be similar to Earth.
                            (12)

2 A Read the article about Professor Marks. Complete the sentences with the present perfect form of the verbs in parentheses.

Glen College: Spotlight on Professor Marks

Professor Andrew Marks _has been_ (be) a professor at Glen College for
(1)

20 years. He _____ (teach) thousands of students in the
(2)

geology department. He ____ _____ (decide) not to retire for
(3)

several years because he loves teaching.

Professor Marks is also a glaciologist. Glaciology is the study of ice and snow.

Professor Marks _____ (looked) at ice from many different glaciers.
(4)

Over the years, Professor Marks _____ (work) for the U.S. Coast Guard and for
(5)

private companies. The U.S. Coast Guard _____ (send) Andrew to the South Pole
(6)

in Antarctica twice. Professor Marks _____ also _____ (travel) to Greenland.
(7)   (7)

In Greenland, Professor Marks _____ (discover) volcanic ash[1] in the ice core
(8)

samples. This ash _____ (show) that a large volcano erupted. Professor Marks
(9)

_____ (publish) articles on his research in many scientific journals.
(10)

[1]**volcanic ash:** the soft gray or black powder ejected from an erupting volcano

B Now write present perfect questions about Professor Marks. Use the answers to help you.

1. **Q:** (who) _Who has Professor Marks taught?_

   A: Professor Marks has taught students in the geology department.

2. **Q:** (why) _____

   A: He has decided not to retire for several years because he loves teaching.

3. **Q:** (who) _____

   A: He has worked for the U.S. Coast Guard and for private companies.

4. **Q:** (how often) _____

   A: The U.S Coast Guard has sent Professor Marks to the South Pole twice.

5. **Q:** (what) _____

   A: He has discovered ash in the ice core samples from Greenland.

6. **Q:** (where) _____

   A: Professor Marks has published articles in many scientific journals.

Present Perfect or Simple Past?

1 Read the classroom discussion about an unplanned discovery. Complete the conversation with the present perfect or simple past form of the verbs in parentheses.

Dr. West: I'd like to talk about the article I assigned yesterday. I'm sure you all __read__ (read) it
(1)
last night.

Irina: Yes, Dr. West. It was interesting, but I'm confused. We _____ (study) scientific
(2)
discoveries in this class a lot this semester. The person in that article isn't a scientist.

Dr. West: Good comment, Irina. Let's think about that. The article was about Terry Herbert.
Who is that? Nick?

Nick: Well, Terry Herbert _____ (be) an amateur[1] treasure hunter for years.
(3)
He _____ (discover) an ancient treasure in England in 2009. Herbert
(4)
_____ (spend) five days searching his friend's field alone. Finally,
(5)
he _____ (realize) he needed help. Professional archeologists then
(6)
_____ (continue) the search. They _____ (find) gold and silver
(7)   (8)
jewelry pieces. Terry Herbert's just an ordinary guy, and he likes to look for metal.

Dr. West: Right. A person sometimes discovers something by accident.[2] _____ you
(9)
_____ (hear) about something like that before? Does anyone remember?
(9)

---

[1]**amateur:** not a professional | [2]**by accident:** unplanned

2 Complete the paragraphs about a crime scene investigation. Use the present perfect or simple past form of the verbs in the boxes.

be	find	look	~~see~~	start

Many people __have seen__ TV shows about the police. They
(1)
know about crime scene[1] investigators (CSIs). For hundreds of years,

investigators _____ for evidence such as fingerprints,
(2)
chemicals, and bits of paper at crime scenes. Police _____
(3)
many criminals because of this evidence. In 1923, Los Angeles

_____ the first police crime laboratory in the United States. Since then, CSIs
(4)

_____ important members of many police departments.
(5)

---

[1]**crime scene:** the place where a crime happened

appear	be	become	do	love	see	use

In 1887, the first story about Sherlock Holmes _____ . Holmes was a fictional[2]
(6)

detective. He _____ CSI methods to find criminals. Everyone _____
(7) (8)

to read stories about him because he _____ very clever and very good at his
(9)

job. He also _____ surprising things to discover the criminals. Today, stories
(10)

about CSIs and their work _____ very popular. _____ you ever
(11) (12)

_____ those CSI shows on TV?
(12)

[2]**fictional:** not true

3 Answer the questions with information that is true for you. Use the present perfect or simple past.

1. What have you discovered about yourself since you started school?

   Since I started school, I have discovered that I like science classes.

2. What did you learn in school last semester?

   _____

3. Where have you been this year?

   _____

4. Where did you go last summer?

   _____

5. Who have you met in your classes this term? Have they become your friends?

   _____

6. Who did you see last week?

   _____

Avoid Common Mistakes

1 Circle the mistakes.

1. I **have had** many great adventures. I **have goed** to Machu Picchu in Peru. Last year I **visited**
   (a)   (b)   (c)
   a Brazilian rain forest.

2. Catherine Coleman **was** in the Air Force. She **has joined** NASA in 1992 and **became** an astronaut.
   (a)   (b)   (c)

3. Mark **has discovered** a box of old letters last year. His great-grandmother **wrote** them
    (a)   (b)
   in the 1920s. He **has read** many of them, and he plans to read more.
                        (c)

4. I **have bought** tickets for my flight to Australia yesterday. I **have read** a lot of travel
     (a)   (b)
   books recently. I **learned** a lot about the country this month.
                          (c)

5. Where **have you been**? What **you have found**? What **have you put** in your pocket?
            (a)   (b)   (c)

6. The police **have beginned** an investigation. They **have brought** several people to the
                  (a)   (b)
   police station and **have gotten** a lot of information.
                            (c)

7. I **bought** a chemistry set last week. I **have tried** an experiment yesterday. It **made**
      (a)   (b)   (c)
   an explosion.

8. What **has Jim found out** about the New York City subways? Where **has he decided** to
          (a)   (b)
   go? What **he has decided** to see?
                (c)

2 Find and correct eight more mistakes in the magazine article about Pluto.

Classifying Pluto

have studied
Scientists ~~studied~~ the night sky for centuries. Astronomers have spended countless hours

studying the sky for new objects. When astronomers have discovered new objects, though,

they have not always agreed what these objects are.

An example of this is the discovery of Pluto. In the early twentieth century, astronomers

have started to suspect that there was a planet beyond Uranus. Then, in 1930, they have

discovered Pluto, and it became the ninth planet. However in 2008, astronomers have

announced that Pluto was no longer a planet. Why they have done this? Pluto is smaller than

any of the other planets. Therefore, astronomers created a new category: "Dwarf Planets."

They are looking for more dwarf planets and have saw several. So far, they found nine.

Self-Assessment

Circle the word or phrase that correctly completes each sentence.

1. *Kaiko* was a robot ship. It _____ Earth's deepest oceans between 1995 and 2003.

   a. has explored   b. have explored   c. explored

2. Where _____ for your lost car keys?

   a. you have looked   b. looked you   c. have you looked

3. Who _____ to be a detective?

   a. has study   b. has studied   c. was studied

4. We understand Egypt's history because researchers _____ many old buildings and artworks.

   a. have found   b. find   c. have

5. I _____ that new adventure movie five times so far this week.

   a. seen   b. saw   c. have seen

6. They like to try different sports. They _____ basketball, soccer, and baseball.

   a. played   b. have played   c. playing

7. _____ watched a bee fly? You've probably discovered that they don't fly very fast.

   a. Have you ever   b. Did you ever   c. You have ever

8. Scientists _____ that humans have at least nine senses, not five. This has affected new research.

   a. agreed have   b. agreed   c. have agreed

9. On February 18, 1930, Clyde Tombaugh _____ a new object in the night sky.

   a. has discovered   b. discovered   c. has

10. This morning, I am cleaning the house. So far, I _____ several coins under the furniture.

    a. have found   b. found   c. have finded

11. I have worked with a few different researchers. Last summer, I _____ at an ancient city in Mexico.

    a. has worked   b. have worked   c. worked

12. We _____ a lot together. For example, we discovered that air travel can be expensive.

    a. has learned   b. have learned   c. haven't learned

13. What new plants _____ on their last trip?

    a. have they discovered   b. they discovered   c. did they discover

14. The number of people who explore the rain forest _____ in this century.

    a. has increased   b. increased   c. has increase

15. We _____ the perfect house to buy last April. Last May, we moved into it.

    a. have found   b. have finded   c. found

Adverbs with Present Perfect

1 Complete the conversation about Easter Island, an island in the South Pacific. Use the adverbs and the present perfect form of the verbs in parentheses.

Julianne: <u>*Have*</u> you <u>*ever heard*</u> (ever / hear) of Easter Island?
　　　　　(1)　　　　　(1)

Daniel: No. I _____ (never / hear) of Easter Island. Where is it? What's
　　　　　　　　　(2)

special about it?

Julianne: It's in the southeastern Pacific Ocean, and it's pretty interesting. Scientists

_____ (still / not / find) the answers to a lot of mysteries on that
　　　(3)

island. Archeologists _____ (already / do) a lot of research on the
　　　　　　　　　(4)

people and the culture. Some scientists think that the original people came

from a Polynesian island, but they _____ (yet / not / prove) it _____ .
(5) (5)

The original people disappeared many years ago. No one knows why, but there

_____ (recently / be) many theories.
(6)

Daniel: That's interesting. What other mysteries _____ scientists
(7)

_____ (lately / study)?
(7)

Julianne: Well, the people of Easter Island built giant stone statues. The statues are not

where they were in the past.

Daniel: Really? _____ scientists _____ (recently / discover) where the
(8) (8)

people built the statues?

Julianne: Yes. Scientists _____ (already / determine) the people carved the
(9)

statues at an extinct volcano.

Daniel: Now the statues are across the island. _____ scientists _____
(10) (10)

(ever / learn) how the people moved the statues?

Julianne: No. Scientists _____ (ever / not / figure) out how the people moved
(11)

the statues.

Daniel: _____ Easter Island _____ (ever / become) popular?
(12) (12)

Julianne: Easter Island _____ (recently / become) a popular tourist place. A
(13)

luxury hotel _____ (just / open), too.
(14)

2 Unscramble the words to make sentences. Use the present perfect form of the verbs.

1. not find / cure for the common cold / yet / Scientists

   Scientists have not found a cure for the common cold yet.

2. However / how to destroy the virus in a lab / learn / recently / they

   _____

3. already / They / some remedies for the common cold / discover

   _____

4. that taking the mineral zinc can help prevent colds / Research / just / show

   _____

5. My friend / recently / tell / me that / eating chicken soup helps

   _____

3 A Storm chasers work for scientists. They follow tornadoes and hurricanes in trucks. Look at the list of tasks that they do before they leave. Write sentences with the words in parentheses and the information in the chart. Use the present perfect form of the verbs.

	Completed
Joe – look at the weather forecasts	✓
Joe – find a storm in the area	✓
Joe – get driving directions to the area	
Sue – put the video cameras in the truck	
Sue – place the laptops in the truck	✓
Sue – fill the gas tank of the truck with gas	
Bob – prepare food	✓
Bob and Joe – organize the truck	✓
Bob – replace batteries in flashlights	✓
Sue and Bob – check the equipment	
Sue and Joe – pack their cell phones	
Bob – buy a first-aid kit	✓

1. (Joe / already / look) <u>*Joe has already looked at the weather forecasts.*</u>

2. (Joe / yet / not get) _____

3. (Sue / already / place) _____

4. (Sue / yet / fill) _____

5. (Bob / already / prepare) _____

6. (Sue and Bob / yet / check) _____

B Write *Yes* / *No* questions and answers. Use the information in A.

1. **A:** Joe / yet / find / a storm in the area?

   <u>*Has Joe found a storm in the area yet?*</u>

   B: <u>*Yes, he has.*</u>

2. **A:** Sue / yet / put / the video cameras / in the truck?

   _____

   B: _____

3. **A:** Bob and Joe / already / organize / the truck?

_____

B: _____

4. **A:** Bob / yet / replace / batteries in flashlights?

_____

B: _____

5. **A:** Sue and Joe / already / pack / their cell phones?

_____

B: _____

6. **A:** Bob / already / buy / a first-aid kit?

_____

B: _____

4 Have you ever heard about these things? Write answers that are true for you. Use the present perfect and *already*, *still*, *yet*, *never*, *just*, *lately*, and *recently* when possible.

1. Mysterious animals

   Yes, I've recently heard of an animal called the Yeti. It is like a gorilla. OR *No, I've*

   never heard of any mysterious animals.

2. The Bermuda Triangle

   _____

3. Butterflies that travel thousands of miles

   _____

4. A very sick person who suddenly became well

   _____

5. Someone who predicts the future

   _____

Present Perfect with *For* and *Since*

1 Complete the phrases with *for* or *since*.

1. ___*for*___ five years
2. _____ she was a child
3. _____ 2010
4. _____ 30 minutes
5. _____ a long time
6. _____ last year
7. _____ then

8. _____ a few days
9. _____ I graduated
10. _____ the 1970s
11. _____ several weeks
12. _____ he was 12 years old
13. _____ they moved to Texas
14. _____ many years

2 A Complete the paragraph about monarch butterflies with *for* or *since*.

The monarch butterflies' migration is another challenge for scientists. In the fall, the

butterflies travel south from Canada and the United States to central Mexico. Then in the

spring, they travel north to the United States again. Scientists have studied this migration

___*for*___ a long time and still have unanswered questions. Alex is one of those scientists.
   (1)

He has lived at the monarch butterfly sanctuary[1] _____ 2005. He has studied the
                                                      (2)

monarchs _____ then. Alex has seen many thousands of monarchs _____ he
          (3)   (4)

came to the sanctuary. The monarch butterflies

survive on their own fat _____ the winter
                          (5)

months. In March, they quickly fly north to lay

their eggs before they die. No one knows how

long they have made this journey. They have

probably done it _____ a very long time.
                  (6)
_____
[1]**sanctuary:** a safe place

B Read the statements about Alex, the scientist in Mexico. Then write questions and answers about his life. Use the present perfect with *for* and *since*.

Alex started to work at the butterfly sanctuary in 2005. He got married eight years ago. He and his wife bought their house five years ago. Alex and his wife began playing music together in 2009.

1. How long / Alex / work / at the butterfly sanctuary?

   Q: _How long has Alex worked at the butterfly sanctuary?_

   A: _He's worked there since 2005._

2. How long / Alex / be / married?

Q: _____

A: _____

3. How long / Alex and his wife / live / in their house?

Q: _____

A: _____

4. How long / Alex and his wife / play / music together?

Q: _____

A: _____

3 Complete the sentences about good lifestyle habits. Write about yourself and people you know. Use the ideas in the box or your own ideas.

be active	exercise	not eat sweets
eat a healthy diet	get plenty of sleep or rest	not drink soda
eat lots of fruit and vegetables	go bike riding	play sports

1. I _haven't drunk soda_____ since _2007_____ .

2. I _____ for _____ .

3. My best friend _____ since _____ .

4. My best friend _____ for _____ .

5. (your own idea) _____

6. (your own idea) _____

Avoid Common Mistakes

1 Circle the mistakes.

1. People **have tried** to explain dreams (since) a long time. They **still** have not explained them.
   (a)   (b)   (c)

2. They have **not never** understood why dreams occur, but **they have done** research **for**
   (a)   (b)   (c)
   many years.

3. Lisa Holland **has studied** dreams **for** last year. She **has just decided** to keep a log of
   (a)   (b)   (c)
   her dreams.

4. Lisa **has started recently** as a lab assistant. She **has worked** there **for** about two months.
   (a)   (b)   (c)

5. Young **is** a researcher at the lab **since** last year. He **has just finished** his first experiment.
    (a)   (b)   (c)

6. I **have never tried** to explain dreams. However, Dr. Chen **has tried** to explain them.
    (a)   (b)

    Unfortunately, his studies **have ever made** any progress.
                                  (c)

7. My professor **has completed** a lot of dream research. **Since** 2009, she **writes** 26 articles.
                  (a)   (b)   (c)

8. We **have learned** a lot about dreams, but we **have ever been** able to explain them **yet**.
       (a)   (b)   (c)

2 Find and correct the mistakes in this article about déjà vu.

Déjà vu and You

Imagine that ~~just~~ you have ^*just* walked into a building for the first time. You have ever been there before. Suddenly, everything feels familiar. You feel like you have been already to this place. We call this feeling *déjà vu*, and it is quite common. Déjà vu is a French expression. It means that you have already seen something, and people use it to talk about experiences they feel they have already had. Seventy percent of the people in surveys say, "Yes, I have experienced it before." Some people experience déjà vu since they were teenagers. Authors have written about this feeling in books since hundreds of years, but scientists have not never explained it. Researchers try to study this feeling for a long time, but they have ever made it happen in a laboratory. As a result, they yet have not been able to understand the déjà vu experience.

Self-Assessment

Circle the word or phrase that correctly completes each sentence.

1. Have you _____ heard of Colony Collapse Disorder?

    a. never   b. yet   c. ever

2. People have researched the history of Easter Island _____ they discovered the statues.

    a. for   b. recently   c. since

3. Mel Green has led a healthy life _____ 85 years.

   a. for   b. since   c. yet

4. We have known about disappearing bees _____ .

   a. for the 1970s   b. since a long time   c. since the 1970s

5. Have the doctors found the cause of that disease _____ ?

   a. recently   b. yet   c. never

6. Researchers have gone to the island ten times _____ .

   a. for 2005   b. since ten years   c. since 2005

7. They have _____ returned from the last research trip.

   a. just   b. lately   c. still

8. Alex _____ has not learned everything about monarch butterflies.

   a. never   b. still   c. yet

9. The scientists have discovered new evidence _____ .

   a. just   b. still   c. lately

10. Melissa has _____ been to Mexico to study monarch butterflies.

    a. recently   b. yet   c. still

11. They have _____ studied bird migration, but they don't know why birds don't get lost.

    a. already   b. still   c. ever

12. Scientists have _____ not found the answers to many mysteries.

    a. lately   b. never   c. still

13. Daniela has been a member of the research team _____ .

    a. since almost five years   b. for almost five years   c. for five years ago

14. The team has studied this problem _____ .

    a. yet   b. still   c. for several months

15. I have _____ seen earthquake lights, and I don't want to!

    a. ever   b. never   c. yet

Present Perfect Progressive

Cities

Present Perfect Progressive

1 Complete the sentences about traffic in the cities. Use the present perfect progressive form of the verbs in parentheses.

1. In cities across the country, the population *has been growing* (grow).

2. Traffic _____ (increase), too.

3. Recently, cities _____ (create) ways to control drivers.

4. Some cities _____ (use) cameras to do this.

5. They _____ (place) cameras at intersections.

6. The cameras _____ (take) pictures of cars that drive through red lights.

7. The police _____ (send) tickets to the drivers of these cars.

8. Drivers _____ (not drive) through as many red lights lately.

2 Complete the questions and answers about Singapore. Use the present perfect progressive form of the verbs in parentheses.

1. **Q:** ___*Have*___ Singaporeans *been living* (live) in the city?

   A: Yes. One hundred percent *have been living* in the city.

2. **Q:** How fast _____ Singapore _____ (develop) since its independence in 1965?

   A: Singapore _____ very fast and attracting many visitors.

3. **Q:** What _____ visitors _____ (come) to see in Singapore?

   A: They _____ to see the Food Festival, the Arts Festival, and the Sun Festival.

4. **Q:** How long _____ the government _____ (advertise) Singapore as a center for arts and culture?

   A: The government _____ Singapore as a center for arts and culture for more than 20 years.

5. **Q:** Where _____ tourists _____ (stay) in Singapore?

   A: They _____ at the many five-star hotels.

3 Answer the questions with information that is true for you. Use the present perfect progressive.

1. Have you been reading the news lately? Where? Online? In a newspaper?

   *Yes. I've been reading the news online.* OR *No. I haven't been reading the*

   *news lately.*

2. What has been happening in the cities of a country you know well recently?

   _____

3. Which cities in a country you know well have been growing the fastest?

   _____

4. What challenges have people been facing in a country you know well?

   _____

Present Perfect Progressive or Present Perfect?

1 A Complete the paragraph about what has been happening in cities around the world. Circle the correct verb forms. Sometimes both verb forms are correct.

All cities have problems, but recently some cities from all around the world

have tried /(have been trying)to find solutions to their environmental problems.
　　　　　　(1)

For example, in Amsterdam, many people **have been riding / have ridden** bicycles
　　　　　　　　　　　　　　　　　　　　　　　　(2)

to reduce traffic and pollution. New York City **has built / has been building**
　　　　　　　　　　　　　　　　　　　　　　　　(3)

a new subway line to improve public transportation. However, the city

has not completed / has not been completing it yet. The people of Curitiba, Brazil,
　　　　　　　　(4)

have understood / have been understanding the importance of being a "green city"
　　　　　　　(5)

for a long time. Some experts estimate that 70 percent of the citizens **have used / have been using** their
(6)
public bus system. There are also many parks. The

city **has hired / has been hiring** a shepherd and his
(7)
sheep to keep the grass short. Vancouver, Canada,

has been / has been being a leader in the use of
(8)
hydroelectric power for a while. There is hope for the future when cities face their

problems and find good solutions.

B Write *Yes / No* questions about the information in A. Use the same form of the verb (present perfect progressive or present perfect) as in A. Then write short answers.

1. some cities / try to find / solutions to their problems?

   Q: *Have some cities been trying to find solutions to some of their problems?*

   A: *Yes, they have.*

2. people in Amsterdam / drive cars / to reduce pollution?

   Q: _____

   A: _____

3. New York City / complete / a new subway line?

   Q: _____

   A: _____

4. people in Curitiba / use / their public bus system?

   Q: _____

   A: _____

5. Curitiba / hire / a shepherd and his sheep?

   Q: _____

   A: _____

6. Vancouver / be / a leader in the use of hydroelectric power?

   Q: _____

   A: _____

2 Read the questions about neighborhood changes. Complete the answers with the present perfect or present perfect progressive form of the verbs in parentheses.

1. What have people been doing with the houses?

   People _have been improving_ (improve) the houses.

2. What has the city been building in this neighborhood?

   The city _____ (build) some green apartments.

3. Where have the residents gone?

   Those people _____ (move into) the city apartments.

4. How has public transportation been improving?

   The city _____ (add) new bus routes.

5. Why has the city made these changes?

   The city _____ (decide) to focus on city-wide improvements.

3 Look at the places in the box. Choose three places to write about in your neighborhood. Describe what has happened or what has been happening.

apartment building(s)	green belt(s)	playground(s)
deli(s)	library(ies)	restaurant(s)
farmers' market(s)	park(s)	shopping mall(s)

1. _The city has started a farmers' market in my neighborhood._

   I have been going there every Saturday for years.

2. _____

   _____

3. _____

   _____

4. _____

   _____

Avoid Common Mistakes

1 Circle the mistakes.

1. The city **has been trying** to improve bus service. The service (**been getting**) better. The
   _(a)   _(b)
   city **has added** four new bus routes.
   _(c)

2. The price of gas **been increasing** since last year. More people **have been riding** city buses.
   _(a)   _(b)   _(c)

3. Police officers **have been knowing** for several years that crime **has been rising** in this area.
   _(a)   _(b) _(c)

4. The situation **has been getting** better. Police officers **are spending** more time in the
   _(a)   _(b)   _(c)
   area since last year.

5. People **been enjoying** new community centers for two years. The city **has**
   _(a)   _(b)
   been building more.
   _(c)

6. The city **is raising** taxes for a few years, and the mayor **has been talking** about another increase.
   _(a)   _(b) _(c)

7. Our city **have been improving** recently. The planning committee **has been creating** green belts.
   _(a) _(b)   _(c)

8. This area **has been changing** a lot recently. It **has been becoming** safer. The city
   _(a)   _(b)
   has been improving this neighborhood.
   _(c)

2 Find and correct eight more mistakes in the paragraph about people without homes.

Homes for the Homeless

　　　　　　　　　has been
Kevin Banks ~~is~~ helping homeless people in his city for a long time. He has been being

a volunteer at the local homeless shelter for 15 years. He is serving meals there since he

was a teenager. The number of homeless people recently been increasing. More people

are losing jobs since last year. The trend is disturbing. For a long time, Kevin has been

believing that the city not been doing enough to solve the problem. Now the city have

been starting new projects to do more. City workers has been building permanent housing

for the homeless. The city has finished more than 300 new apartments for the homeless.

Self-Assessment

Circle the word or phrase that correctly completes each sentence.

1. Allison _____ in traffic for the last 30 minutes.

   a. has been sitting   b. is sitting   c. has sitting

2. Megumi _____ to work lately.

    a. has not walking   b. has not been walking   c. have not walked

3. How long _____ as a police officer for the city?

    a. Luis been working   b. has Luis work   c. has Luis been working

4. My wife and I _____ about getting an apartment downtown.

    a. been talking   b. have been talking   c. has been talking

5. Hyun-Ju _____ with her cousin since she arrived in the city.

    a. has stay   b. have stayed   c. has been staying

6. My parents will never move. They _____ in this city since I was a child.

    a. have been living   b. has lived   c. been living

7. Jared _____ a city employee for about two months.

    a. have been being   b. is being   c. has been

8. Beatriz _____ five classes at the local community college.

    a. has been taking   b. have taken   c. been taking

9. The urban planners _____ the plans for the new green building.

    a. have already finished   b. has been finishing   c. have already been finishing

10. Lorena _____ the bus to work since her car broke down.

    a. been riding   b. has been riding   c. has riding

11. I _____ two really interesting books about urban design lately.

    a. have reading   b. been reading   c. have been reading

12. _____ a lot of time in the new public library downtown?

    a. You been spending   b. Have you been spending   c. You have spending

13. Our city _____ a lot since 2000.

    a. is changing   b. been changing   c. has been changing

14. **A:** Have people been using the new public transportation system? **B:** _____ .

    a. Yes, they have   b. Yes, they do   c. No, they aren't

15. _____ about the problem for a long time?

    a. Have the planners   b. Have the planners   c. Has the planners
       been knowing   known   been knowing

Adjectives
A Good Workplace

Adjectives

1 Unscramble the sentences about young workers. Be sure to put the adjective in the correct place in the sentence.

1. Many / are / people / workers / young   *Many young people are workers.*

2. have / part-time / They / jobs / often   _____

3. wages / low / They / earn   _____

4. hours / don't work / long / They   _____

5. work schedules / are / Their / short   _____

6. simple / job training / is / Their / usually   _____

7. Their / usually / are / jobs / not stressful   _____

8. is / workplace / safe / usually / Their   _____

2 Rewrite the sentences about a new computer company. Put the adjective before the noun. Add *a* or *an* when necessary.

1. The computer company is ethical.

   It is _an ethical computer company_____.

2. The computer company is safe.

   It is _____.

3. The offices are comfortable.

They are _____ .

4. The equipment isn't dangerous.

It isn't _____ .

5. The employees work 35 hours a week.

They have _____ .

6. The employees receive pay for overtime.

They receive _____ .

7. The employees get training for free.

They get _____ .

8. The employees are satisfied.

They are _____ .

3 Match nouns from Columns A and B. Complete the sentences about clothes in the workplace.

A	B
business	classes
career	clothes
running	~~environment~~
training	goals
work	shoes
~~workplace~~	uniform

1. To succeed in the _workplace_ _environment_ , you should follow some guidelines.

2. For an office job, wear _____ _____ , such as a suit, skirt, or dress.

3. Wear nice shoes. Don't wear _____ _____ to the office.

4. In other jobs, such as in hospitals, the management may give you a _____ _____ to wear. You won't wear your own clothes.

5. Make sure to go to any _____ _____ that your company offers. They will improve your skills.

6. Work hard and do your best. Those are excellent _____ _____ in any workplace.

4 Complete the e-mail with the adjectives in parentheses.

send | attach | save draft | forward | close

From: Dina Jackman <djackman87@cambridge.org>
To: Ana Chen <anachen94@cambridge.org>
Subject: My New Job

Hi Ana,

I just love my new job! My _big comfortable_ (comfortable / big) office is on
                              (1)
the 45th floor of a _____ (new / glass) building. I have
                              (2)
_____ (large / nice) windows with a view of the city. Today, I
              (3)
can see a _____ (blue / beautiful / Chicago) sky.
                          (4)
I have a _____ (wooden / round / black)
                      (5)
desk with a _____ (leather / super / black)
                          (6)
chair. I know it's silly to talk about these things. I should tell you about the

_____ (five-hour / training / free) course they
              (7)
are giving me, but I like telling you about my office better.

Best,
Dina

5 Write statements about your workplace or your school. Use two or more adjectives before a noun when possible.

1. _My workplace is a large busy restaurant._

   I have met some interesting young co-workers there.

2. _____

   _____

3. _____

   _____

4. _____

   _____

5. _____

   _____

More About Adjectives

1 Complete the paragraph about job satisfaction. Write the correct adjective ending: *-ed* or *-ing*.

What makes people feel excit_ed_ about their jobs? Researchers asked employees this
 (1)

question. Some of their answers were surpris____ . For many employees, their work is most
 (2)

important to them. Workers want to have challeng____ work. They don't like a bor____
 (3)   (4)

job. When employees feel bor____ , it can make them depress____ about going to work.
 (5)   (6)

Workers also want job security. They don't want to lose their jobs. They also get confus____
 (7)

when there are too many changes in management. Then they start to worry. Workers also

like to control most of their work time. It is very frustrat____ to have a supervisor who checks
 (8)

on you every minute. Finally, workers want a safe workplace. Employees can't do their best

work if the managers are not interest____ in their safety or have policies that discriminate.
 (9)

2 Rewrite the sentences. Replace the nouns in bold with *one* or *ones*.

1. You wore your red shoes to work yesterday, so you should wear the brown **shoes** today.

   You wore your red shoes to work yesterday, _so you should wear the brown ones today_ .

2. My co-workers tell boring jokes, but my boss tells really funny **jokes**.

   My co-workers tell boring jokes, _____ .

3. Would you rather work at a formal office or at a casual **office**?

   Would you rather work at a formal office _____ ?

4. Abby has annoying coworkers, but her roommate has friendly **coworkers**.

   Abby has annoying coworkers, _____ .

5. Topher wants to hire the younger applicant, even though the older **applicant** is more
   qualified.

   Topher wants to hire the younger applicant, _____ .

6. Mercy wants to buy headphones for work. She's looking at some noise-canceling
   headphones.

   Mercy wants to buy headphones for work. _____ .

7. I'm buying new furniture for my office. Do you like the leather chair or the wood **chair** better?

   I'm buying new furniture for my office. Do you like the leather chair or

   _____ ?

3 Read the paragraph about Debby's new job. Then complete the answers. Use the questions and the words in parentheses to help you.

Debby likes her new boss. His name is Bob Martin. He is 55, but he acts much younger. He is an accountant. She is excited about working for him. He tells really funny jokes. Debby feels happy and laughs a lot. Her boss also has done some surprising things. Yesterday, he brought breakfast to work. There was something delicious for everyone. He has nothing negative to say about Debby's work. In fact, he says her work makes him proud. Now she is interested in taking some accounting courses. She is aware of a new course that starts next week. Debby wants to stay with the company and with her boss.

1. How old is Debby's boss?

    He is _55 years old_ (number + measurement word + adjective).

2. What kind of jokes does he tell?

    He tells funny _____ (pronoun).

3. How does she feel about the jokes?

    The jokes make her _____ (adjective).

4. What did they have for breakfast yesterday?

    Everyone had _____ (pronoun + adjective).

5. What does Mr. Martin say about Debby's work?

    He doesn't say _____ (pronoun + adjective) about it.

6. How does Debby's boss feel about her work?

    It makes him _____ (adjective).

7. What accounting course is Debby aware of?

    She is aware of a new _____ (pronoun) that starts next week.

8. What is your opinion of Mr. Martin?

    He seems like a _____ (adjective) boss.

4 Write sentences about your life or work with the words in parentheses. Use the adjectives in the box or your own ideas.

amazing	frustrating	important	new	unusual
annoying	good	interesting	special	

1. (something) *I learned something new yesterday.*

2. (anything) *There isn't anything more important than my health.*

3. (something) _____

4. (anything) _____

5. (nothing) _____

Avoid Common Mistakes

1 Circle the mistakes.

1. Yi has a **terrible** job and an **awfull** boss. She is a **21-year-old** woman with
   (a)   (b)   (c)
   no experience.

2. After a **three-hour** meeting, Irina felt very **stressed**. She wanted to **relaxed**.
   (a)   (b)   (c)

3. I have to work **60-hours** weeks for a **big advertising** company. My job is very **stressful**.
   (a)   (b)   (c)

4. Dina has a **new beautiful** office in a **62-story** building. She is very **excited** about it.
   (a)   (b)   (c)

5. Jake took a **three-day** course to learn how to use the **great new** software. It was
   (a)   (b)
   very **usefull**.
   (c)

6. The **relaxed young** man gave a **20-minutes** talk about how to handle a
   (a)   (b)
   stressful workplace.
   (c)

7. Mira's **careful** explanation was clear. Her **23-year-old** assistant was not **worry** at all.
   (a)   (b)   (c)

8. Burak works a **30-hour** week as a **trained** nurse. He takes care of **an old nice** man in
   (a)   (b)   (c)
   his home.

2 Find and correct eight more mistakes in the article about the best American companies.

The 150 Best Companies to Work For

interested

If you are ~~interest~~ in finding a great company to work for, *Excel in Your Job* magazine can be a good source of information. Every year, the magazine makes a list of the best companies to work for. What makes these companies so successfull? How do they create a workplace good environment? Some companies let employees work four-days weeks so they can have longer weekends with their families. Companies on the list sometimes offer financial excellent benefits, such as high salaries, bonus pay, and retirement plans. Also, employees of these companies are not worry about losing their jobs. They believe their bosses are fair and their rights are protected. It is not unusual to find an employee who has a 30-years career with one of these companies. The list includes small companies as well as giant corporations. No matter what size or location you are interest in, the list can be helpfull.

Self-Assessment

Circle the word or phrase that correctly completes each sentence.

1. Mari Nakajima is _____ .

   a. a responsible   b. an employee responsible   c. a responsible employee

2. Many _____ have offices in Chicago.

   a. international   b. companies   c. internationals
      companies   internationals   companies

3. **A:** Which chemicals are unsafe and illegal? **B:** _____ .

   a. The toxics   b. The toxic ones   c. The toxics ones

4. Sometimes Marcelo's jokes _____ .

   a. are annoy   b. are annoyed   c. are annoying

5. Does Brandon understand the instructions? He seems _____ .

   a. confused   b. confuse   c. confusing

6. How many _____ have you filled out this week?

   a. jobs applications   b. job applications   c. applications job

7. In July, Ji Sung is taking _____ .

   a. a two-weeks vacation   b. two-weeks vacations   c. a two-week vacation

8. After a stressful day at work, Yuri likes to take _____ shower.

   a. a nice long   b. a long nice   c. long nice

9. Rajat had _____ week at work.

   a. a easy   b. an easy   c. easy

10. Meeting new co-workers _____ .

    a. makes nervous   b. nervous some   c. makes some
       some people   people makes   people nervous

11. Our office building is only _____ .

    a. 100 high feet   b. 100 feet high   c. 100 feets high

12. Sharon didn't learn _____ at the training session yesterday.

    a. any new   b. new anything   c. anything new

13. Jessica and Meg are _____ in the office this week. Everyone else is at a conference.

    a. alones   b. alone   c. alone ones

14. Thien's factory job _____ . There are too many toxic chemicals.

    a. makes him sick   b. makes sick him   c. makes sick

15. The new employee is _____ . She has told us a lot about her trips.

    a. interesting   b. interested   c. interest

Adverbs of Manner and Degree

Learn Quickly!

Adverbs of Manner

1 Write the adverb form of the adjectives.

1. clear	_clearly_	7. careful	_____	13. polite	_____
2. fast	_____	8. nervous	_____	14. early	_____
3. alone	_____	9. right	_____	15. terrible	_____
4. good	_____	10. sudden	_____	16. hard	_____
5. quick	_____	11. high	_____	17. low	_____
6. wrong	_____	12. easy	_____	18. usual	_____

2 Complete the article about sleep and learning with the adverb form of the adjective in parentheses.

Scientists have found that people need to sleep _soundly_ (sound) before they learn
(1)

something new. However, students often stay up _____ (late) to study the
(2)

night before a test. The brain handles learning in a similar way to memories. Therefore, the

brain needs time to store the learning _____ (proper).
(3)

In a research study, scientists gave students

a task. The students practiced doing the task

_____ (careful) for an hour. When
(4)

students did the task later the same day, there was

no improvement. After six to eight hours of sleep,

however, the students finished the task much more

_____ (quick). Students who slept for
(5)

less than six hours didn't show any improvement.

Why not? People sleep _____ (different) at the beginning and end of the
(6)
night. People sleep _____ (deep) during the first two hours of sleep. After
(7)
the first two hours of sleep, the brain _____ (slow) makes connections, and
(8)
memories become stronger. In the final two hours of sleep, the brain continues to review

new information and store it. People need all of these kinds of sleep in order to learn

_____ (efficient). As a result, in addition to studying, it is important for
(9)
students to sleep _____ (good) to do their best.
(10)

3 Complete the sentences about learning styles. Use the correct forms of the words in
parentheses. Write one adverb and one adjective for each number.

1. (different) People learn _differently_ . They have _different_ learning styles, which means

   they use different strategies to learn.

2. (careful) Some learners do better when they follow directions _____ .

   Other learners don't like to be _____ about directions.

3. (neat) My friend's desk is always _____ . He can study only after he has

   arranged everything _____ .

4. (good) Some people are "aural" learners – they learn best from what they hear. These

   people are usually _____ listeners. Other people listen but don't learn

   _____ .

5. (calm) Some people are "kinesthetic" learners – they learn when they move around.

   They don't feel _____ when they sit for a long time. Others can sit

   _____ in their seats and learn easily.

6. (clear) Some people are "visual" learners. A learner sees a diagram or picture, and then

   ideas become _____ . They don't understand ideas _____

   when they only hear them.

7. (good) Some students learn _____ in groups. Others do a

   _____ job alone.

8. (quiet) Does everyone learn best in a _____ place? No. Many students get

   nervous when everyone around them is sitting _____ . They concentrate

   better if there is noise and music.

4 Answer the questions with information that is true for you. Use adverbs of manner.

1. Do you learn easily from what you hear? How do you know?

   No, I don't. I often ask people to repeat information clearly.

2. Do you learn easily from what you see? How do you know?

   _____

3. Do you like to move around when you learn something?

   _____

4. How do you remember what you have learned?

   _____

Adverbs of Degree

1 Rewrite the sentences about Lucy. Add the adverb of degree in parentheses.

1. Lucy was concerned about her writing. (terribly)

   Lucy was terribly concerned about her writing.

2. She was worried about failing English. (seriously)

   _____

   _____

3. She was close to dropping the course. (dangerously)

   _____

   _____

4. The teachers at the Writing Center have been helpful. (amazingly)

   _____

5. They are supportive. (wonderfully)

   _____

6. Her progress was good to pass the test. (enough)

   _____

7. She is proud of herself. (incredibly)

   _____

2 Complete the conversation between Professor Meyers and Miguel. Circle the correct words.

Dr. Meyers: Make sure you read chapter six (carefully enough) / too carefully tonight. There will be a
quiz tomorrow. Don't read it **quickly enough / too quickly** though, or you won't do well
on the quiz. That's all for today, class.

Miguel: Dr. Meyers, could I speak with you privately? I don't think I'm doing well in class.

Dr. Meyers: I see. Well, your grades were **good enough / too good** at the beginning of the semester,
but you didn't do very well on your last paper. Your paper was **short enough / too short**.

Miguel: I understand, Dr. Meyers. I was sort of embarrassed to turn in that last paper. I started
writing the paper **late enough / too late**. So it wasn't **long enough / too long**.

Dr. Meyers: I know it's hard to balance work and school, but I know that you can do it. If you study
hard enough / too hard, you will be able to improve your grades. You just have to
organize your time.

3 Rewrite the sentences. Make the formal adverbs in bold more informal. Don't change the
strength of the adverb. Sometimes more than one answer is possible.

1. Marc thinks his world history class is **quite** interesting.

   Marc thinks his world history class is really interesting.

2. The professor is **extremely** intelligent.

3. Marc's study group is **rather** serious.

4. Marc has been doing **fairly** well in the class.

5. He is **rather** proud of his writing.

6. Marc is **somewhat** surprised that he likes world history.

7. He is **somewhat** serious about his history studies.

8. Marc's grades are **extremely** good in both world history and English.

Avoid Common Mistakes

1 Circle the mistakes.

1. Do you remember names (easy)? It can be **incredibly** **difficult**.
   (a)   (b)   (c)

2. Here are a few **easy** tips that can help you learn new names **really** **good**.
   (a)   (b)   (c)

3. Listen **carefully** to the person you meet. Sometimes they say **clearly** their names, but we
   (a)   (b)

   don't listen **well**.
   (c)

4. When we don't **kind of** focus on an introduction, we don't **really** hear the name **well**.
   (a)   (b)   (c)

5. Say the new name **immediately** after you hear it. Then you can be **sure** you heard it **correct**.
   (a)   (b)   (c)

6. Sometimes a person says his or her name **very** **quick**. You can ask him or her to say it again
   (a)   (b)

   more **slowly**.
   (c)

7. Sometimes you don't hear the name **very** **clearly**. Ask **politely** the person to say the name again.
   (a)   (b)   (c)

8. You can ask people to spell their names when you aren't **absolutely** **certain** you heard
   (a)   (b)

   them **rightly**.
   (c)

2 Find and correct eight more mistakes in the paragraph about comfortable classrooms.

Comfortable Classrooms for Better Learning

A comfortable classroom environment is important for students to learn a language
well
~~good~~. When students don't feel somewhat comfortable, they can't learn effective. Good

teachers don't make students feel embarrassed when they answer incorrect. Students also

feel more comfortable when teachers don't speak too fastly. Teachers should treat fairly all

students and make sure that the communication in the classroom is respectful. In a good

classroom, students treat respectfully their classmates even when they serious disagree. In

an effective classroom, both the teacher and the students want each other to do good.

Self-Assessment

Circle the word or phrase that correctly completes each sentence.

1. Lorena thought the history test seemed quite _____ .

   a. hardly   b. easily   c. easy

2. Chao has been doing very _____ in his English courses.

   a. good   b. well   c. goodly

3. The lecture was _____ .

    a. long too   b. enough long   c. too long

4. Because the instructions weren't _____ , several students were confused.

    a. pretty clear   b. very clear   c. somewhat clear

5. Meena's children learned English _____ because they moved here at a very young age.

    a. real quick   b. quite quickly   c. very fastly

6. Roberto doesn't like working in groups. He prefers to work _____ .

    a. alone   b. independent   c. lonely

7. Ken _____ before the final exam.

    a. carefully his notes   b. studied carefully   c. studied his notes
       studied   his notes   carefully

8. The teacher called on Irina. She seemed nervous, but she answered _____ .

    a. the question correct   b. the question correctly   c. correctly the question

9. Thuy is really quiet in class, but she is _____ .

    a. incredibly friendly   b. incredible friend   c. incredible friendly

10. Felipe uses different techniques to communicate _____ .

    a. more effective   b. more effectively   c. too effectively

11. Pablo stayed up _____ to finish his assignment for class.

    a. real lately   b. really lately   c. very late

12. Sebastian _____ .

    a. answered the question   b. answered thoughtfully   c. answered the
       thoughtfully   the question   question thoughtful

13. The teacher speaks _____ for all of the students to understand her.

    a. clear enough   b. clearly enough   c. enough clearly

14. Dmitri doesn't like to speak in class, but he _____ .

    a. writes beautiful   b. beautifully writes   c. writes beautifully

15. I think these questions are _____ .

    a. too hard   b. too hardly   c. too hardly enough

Prepositions

Food on the Table

Prepositions of Place and Time

1 Complete the sentences with the prepositions in the box. Sometimes more than one answer
is possible.

at	during	for	in	in	on
during	~~for~~	in	in	near	

For several years, scientists _____ Iowa State University asked, "How far do fruit
(1)   (2)

and vegetables usually travel? What happens to them on this journey?" They studied the

fruit and vegetables _____ some supermarket shelves _____ Chicago. _____
                        (3)   (4)   (5)

2001, the scientists reported the average distance that fruit and vegetables travel: 1,518

miles. The average apple travels _____ a box on a truck _____ three or four
                                  (6)   (7)

days. _____ that time, the apple can hit others _____ it. Sometimes apples get
        (8)   (9)

damaged _____ the journey. Shoppers _____ the supermarket will not buy them.
          (10)   (11)

2 Complete the sentences about ways to protect fruit. Circle the correct prepositions.

1. Fruit can get damaged (during)/ **since** the long journey to a supermarket.

2. For example, grapes placed **in / under** heavy things in an airplane can get damaged.

3. How can people protect fruit that travels **at / in** an airplane?

4. **Before / For** years, processing plants used special packages.

5. Each kind of fruit was **in / on** its own soft package.

6. You can see apples in these packages **at / behind** some supermarkets.

7. **After / Before** a few years, scientists found cheaper ways to protect fruit.

8. Scientists produced fruit with tougher skin. This fruit began appearing **at / on** supermarket shelves.

9. These new kinds of fruit did not become damaged **during / near** a trip to the market.

10. **For / Since** the early 1990s, most supermarkets have sold only tough-skinned fruit.

11. The fruit has great taste **under / at** its tough skin.

3 Look at the pictures. Complete the answers with the words in the boxes. Add *the* when necessary.

A Jin-Sun finishes breakfast.

| ~~7:30~~ | in | refrigerator |
| ~~before~~ | on | table |

1. When did Jin-Sun finish breakfast?

   She finished *before 7:30* .

2. Where did she put the milk container?

   She put it _____ .

3. Where did she leave the bananas?

   She left them _____ .

B Gabriel goes to work.

| afternoon | behind | in |
| at | Food Place | truck |

4. Where does Gabriel work?

   He works _____ .

5. Where is the car?

   It is _____ .

6. It is not morning. When does he go to work?

   He goes to work _____ .

C Nicole goes food shopping.

box	next to	shelf
in	on	tomatoes

7. Where are the tomatoes?

They are _____.

8. Where are the potatoes?

They are _____.

9. Where are the carrots?

They are _____.

4 Write answers that are true for you. Use prepositions of place and time.

1. What country do you live in?

 I live in the United States. _____

2. How long have you lived there?

 _____

3. Where do you buy your food?

 _____

4. What day do you usually shop?

 _____

5. How long do you usually shop?

 _____

6. At the supermarket, where do you pay for your food?

 _____

7. Where do you put milk and eggs at home?

 _____

8. What do you do with extra food you can't eat?

 _____

Prepositions of Direction and Manner

1 Complete the sentences about where we grow different kinds of food. Circle the correct prepositions.

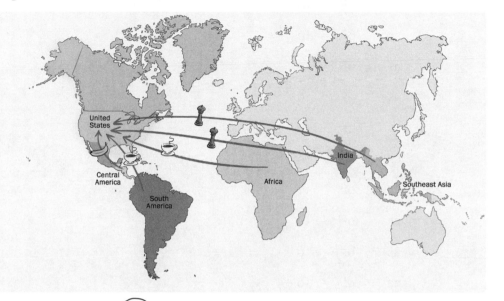

1. Some food comes **(from)** / **over** distant places because it cannot grow locally.

2. Ships bring bananas **about / to** the United States from Central America.

3. They transport black pepper **across / around** the ocean from India and Southeast Asia.

4. Many people in the United States start their day **with / as** coffee from Africa or South America.

5. Now, scientists can produce new kinds of plants **for / into** farmers.

6. They can grow all **between / around** the world.

7. Now, a larger part **as / of** our food can come from local farmers.

2 Complete the paragraph about locavores with the prepositions in the box.

across	for	from	from	to	~~from~~	of	to

A *locavore* is a person who prefers to eat local food *from* farmers' markets or
_____ his or her own garden. Locavores believe their food tastes better because it has
not traveled _____ the ocean. It is very fresh and more nutritious than food that goes
_____ the supermarket. Most supermarket food travels thousands _____ miles
_____ many days. Locavores want to help the environment with their food choices.
Many locavores will go _____ an area a little farther away from their communities
only if necessary. The important thing is that by creating a boundary, no matter how large,
they are becoming more aware of where their food comes _____ .

(1) ... (8)

Phrasal Prepositions and Prepositions After Adjectives

1 A Circle the correct words to complete the phrasal prepositions.

1. because __*of*__   as   (of)   to

2. close _____   as   of   to

3. in front _____   as   of   to

4. such _____   as   of   to

5. up _____   as   of   to

6. next _____   as   of   to

7. instead _____   as   of   to

8. outside _____   as   of   to

9. as well _____   as   of   to

10. out _____   as   of   to

B Complete the paragraphs. Use the phrasal prepositions from items 1–4 in A in the first paragraph. Use the phrasal prepositions from items 5–8 in A in the second paragraph.

Companies build their supermarkets in special ways. This is _*because of*_ what
(1)

shoppers like, _____ open space in the store. To create open space, store
(2)

owners do not put one shelf too _____ another. They want shoppers to see
(3)

everything. They do not put big things _____ small things.
(4)

Store owners want shoppers to move easily around a supermarket. Customers don't

like to carry food or take carts _____ a second floor. _____
(5)   (6)

a second floor, supermarkets have only one level. Also, when shoppers go

_____ the store to their cars, they do not like to walk far. This is why
(7)

owners build big parking lots _____ their stores.
(8)

2 A Complete the questions. Write the prepositions that come after the adjectives in bold.
Use prepositions in the box.

about	~~by~~	for	from	of	to	with

1. When you walk into a supermarket, what are you **surprised** _by_ ?

2. What food is **good** _____ you?

3. What good things are vegetables **full** _____ ?

4. When you buy food, what are you **worried** _____ ?

5. What farmers' markets in your area are you **familiar** _____ ?

6. Do you think local food tastes **different** _____ supermarket food?

7. What are high food prices **due** _____ ?

B Write answers to the questions in A. Write sentences that are true for you.

1. _I'm surprised by the poor quality of the produce._____

2. _____

3. _____

4. _____

5. _____

6. _____

7. _____

Avoid Common Mistakes

1 Circle the mistakes.

1. There are farmers' markets **in** most cities. My favorite one is (at) New York City. It's one of
   (a)   (b)
   the largest **in** the United States.
   (c)

2. I go shopping **on** Sundays. I work **on** the other days. I don't like shopping **in** my one
   (a)   (b)   (c)
   free day.

3. Kelly lives **next to** a candy store. Candy is **bad for** her children. She is **worried of**
   (a)   (b)   (c)
   what they eat.

4. Apples stay fresh **since** two months. Bananas stay fresh **for** a day. No fruit stays fresh **for** a year.
   (a)   (b)   (c)

5. I was **surprised by** the smell in my house. Was it **due to** the refrigerator? The refrigerator was
   (a)   (b)
   full by old food.
   (c)
6. Some trees live **for** 1,000 years. Some live **during** 100 years. Others live **for** only 10 years.
              (a)   (b)   (c)
7. I shop at a market **in** my town. I think it's the best one **at** the state. Maybe it's the best
                      (a)   (b)
   in the country!
   (c)
8. **In** July 25, I'm having a party. I'm picking up a cake **on** Friday. The party starts **at** 7:00 p.m.
   (a)   (b)   (c)

2 Find and correct eight more mistakes in the paragraph about healthy eating.

Healthy Food

                                                            for
Author Michael Pollan has written about local food ~~during~~ many years. He lives at

California at the United States. He grows his vegetables in his garden. He believes that

Americans do not eat enough fruit and vegetables. He also believes some health problems

are due from bad food choices. He says that we have been eating bad food since too long.

However, many Americans say that they are too busy to spend much time thinking about

their food choices. They work long hours. Sometimes they work at Saturdays and Sundays

or on holidays. They do not have time to cook all of their meals. They do not have time to

go to farmers' markets in Saturdays. They eat quick and easy food that is not good with

them. Michael Pollan writes about food to get people excited in healthier ways to eat.

Self-Assessment

Circle the word or phrase that correctly completes each sentence.

1. Trucks take tomatoes from Florida _____ New York.

   a. to   b. for   c. since

2. When you put a bad apple _____ good ones, they all go bad.

   a. next to   b. instead of   c. outside of

3. I'm excited _____ my mother's special fruit salad. It's delicious.

   a. with   b. of   c. about

4. My roommate pays the phone bill. I am responsible _____ the grocery bill.

   a. from   b. to   c. for

5. Food explorers travel _____ forests and jungles to find new kinds of food.

   a. from   b. through   c. at

6. You can't find shopping carts behind stores. People get them _____ of stores.

   a. because   b. instead   c. in front

7. When food gets too old, store owners throw it _____ the trash.

   a. in   b. across   c. through

8. Coffee grows in these mountains. It grows _____ the northern part to the far south.

   a. since   b. from   c. to

9. People in the United States throw away 200,000 tons _____ food each day.

   a. at   b. of   c. for

10. Green vegetables _____ as lettuce and broccoli are important.

    a. aware   b. instead   c. such

11. These vegetables are full _____ natural chemicals that keep you healthy.

    a. of   b. from   c. with

12. It is bad for you to eat snacks and sugary food _____ of fresh fruit and vegetables.

    a. because   b. outside   c. instead

13. Sometimes, the price of food goes up _____ to bad weather on farms.

    a. because   b. due   c. close

14. Some food goes _____ processing plants. The workers clean and package it.

    a. through   b. over   c. outside

15. Strawberries are similar _____ oranges. They both have lots of vitamin C.

    a. through   b. with   c. to

Art Credits

Illustration

Edwin Fotheringham: 10, 95, 100, 164; **Andrew NG:** 43, 106, 138, 146, 169; **John Kurtz:** 52, 158, 204; **Foo Lim:** 78, 95, 101, 110

Photography

2 *(l)* ©Elwynn*, *(r)* ©iStockphoto.com/STEEX; 12 Bruce Laurance/Getty Images; 13 iStockphoto.com/kali9; 16 ©iStockphoto.com/philsajonesen; 23 Jupiterimages/Getty Images; 24 Bloomberg via Getty Images; 29 DEA Picture Library/Getty Images; 31 *(l)* IndexStock/SuperStock, *(r)* ©Neelsky*; 34 *(l)* Chris McGrath/Getty Images, *(r)* Mandel Ngan/AFP/Getty Images; 35 2011 STAR TRIBUNE/Minneapolis-St. Paul; 36 ©Kevin Tavares*; 37 David Karp/Ap Images; 50 Digital Globe/ZUMA/Corbis; 57 Bill Haber/AP Images; 59 Barry Austin/Getty Images; 64 Courtesy of Jet Propulsion Laboratory; 65 National Geographic/Getty Images; 66 Imagebroker.net/Superstock; 70 ©Tomaz Kunst*; 71 Jim Reed/Getty Images; 74 ©Sari Oneal*; 78 Andrew Watson/Photolibrary; 80 ©iStockphoto.com/wekeli; 81 Keith Bedford/Corbis; 84 Moodboard/Corbis; 88 Michael Maslan/Corbis; 92 Bill Varie/Corbis; 98 ©Paula Cobleigh*; 110 Newspix/Getty Images; 112 Yellow Dog Productions/Getty Images; 115 ©iStockphoto.com/4774344sean; 118 ©Shpilko Dmitriy*; 120 ©Susan Schmitz*; 124 Handout/Getty Images; 127 Filmmagic/Getty Images; 134 *(l)* ©iStockphoto.com/ArtisticCaptures, *(c)* ©Monkey Business Images*, *(r)* ©Stocklite*; 160 Corbis Super RF/Alamy; 166 ©iStockphoto.com/opulent-images; 171 Christopher Bissell/Getty Images; 176 Masterfile Royalty Free; 179 *(l)* ©Warren Goldswain*, *(r)* ©iStockphoto.com/billnoll; 184 *(t)*Reuters/Corbis, *(b)* ©iStockphoto.com/NetaDegany; 185 Comstock/Getty Images; 190 ©Korionov*; 193 Jose Luis Pelaez/Corbis; 197 Steve Hix/Getty Images; 198 *(t)* ©iStockphoto.com/tuncaycetin, *(b)* H. Armstrong Roberts/The Image Works; 204 Barcroft/Fame Pictures; 208 ©Sebastian Kaulitzki*; 209 ©topseller*; 214 Courtesy of The Pirate Guys LLC; 215 ©iStockphoto.com/dlewis33; 216 ©iStockphoto.com/wwing; 217 Floyd Dean/Getty Images.

*2011 Used under license from Shutterstock.com